C000080860

Public Speaking

Vivian Summers was educated at the universities of Exeter and Cambridge. He was Head of the English Department at Queen Elizabeth School, Crediton, for over thirty years. He has also lectured at a college of education and at the International Summer Schools held at Exeter University. He has been appointed a Visiting Assessor in the subject for one of the GCSE Examining Groups and he is an examiner for the English Speaking Board, of which he is a Fellow. He is also a freelance writer with several books on English to his credit.

ADVISORY EDITORS: Stephen Coote and Bryan Loughrey

Public Speaking

Vivian Summers

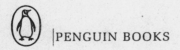 PENGUIN BOOKS

PENGUIN BOOKS

Published by the Penguin Group
27 Wrights Lane, London W8 5TZ, England
Viking Penguin Inc., 40 West 23rd Street, New York, New York 10010, USA
Penguin Books Australia Ltd, Ringwood, Victoria, Australia
Penguin Books Canada Ltd, 2801 John Street, Markham, Ontario, Canada L3R 1B4
Penguin Books (NZ) Ltd, 182–190 Wairau Road, Auckland 10, New Zealand

Penguin Books Ltd, Registered Offices: Harmondsworth, Middlesex, England

First published 1988

Typeset, printed and bound in Great Britain by
Hazell Watson & Viney Limited,
Member of the BPCC Group,
Aylesbury, Bucks

Typeset in Linotron 202 Melior

Contents

6   Contents

Acknowledgements

I acknowledge with gratitude the specialist advice readily given to me by Sir Peter Mills, Canon Bruce Duncan, Professor W. P. Jolly and Mrs Kathleen Wareham. To my wife and family I offer my grateful thanks for their support and encouragement during the writing of this book.

V.S.

Author's Note

To avoid the repetition in the text of cumbersome phrases such as 'he or she', 'him or her' etc., masculine forms frequently have been used. This in no way implies that public speaking is a male preserve. I hope the book will be of use to both men and women public speakers.

Introduction

The toastmaster, resplendent in his red jacket, raps the table with his gavel. 'My Lords, Ladies and Gentlemen, pray silence for . . .' There is prolonged applause as the eminent visitor rises to his feet and smiles confidently down the long rows of tables. A distinguished company sits happily relaxed after a sumptuous banquet. The glasses have been refilled, the cigar smoke curls upward. The after-dinner speeches have begun.

This is something like the mental picture we all have when the words 'public speaking' are mentioned. We think of an important formal occasion when the speaker entertains a large company with his wit and oratory, perhaps impressing his audience with a devastating analysis of public affairs or having them rolling with mirth at his fund of stories and carefully calculated asides.

How we all long to have the skill and confidence to command an audience in this way! But is this really what public speaking is all about? There must be very few people who will ever find themselves in such a situation, addressing a grand audience in a banqueting hall in the full blaze of publicity. Yet there are numerous occasions on which any one of us may be invited to stand up in front of a group of people and say something to them. It may be a simple announcement in a village hall, a speech at a wedding, a report on a project to a group of fellow businessmen, a talk about one's job to a class of teenagers or some remarks at a colleague's retirement ceremony. All these, and many more, involve public speaking, and all of them can strike terror into the heart of the inexperienced person who is invited to 'come along and say a few words'.

Yet the ability to speak in public can be acquired by those who are prepared to make the effort to think hard about what they are doing and to practise. Some people have a natural gift for this sort of thing, while for others the mere thought of speaking to an audience is a nightmare. Undoubtedly the greatest problem for many would-be speakers is – nerves. It is so much of a problem that a whole chapter of this book will be devoted to it. Let's just say for the moment that nerves can be conquered by knowing what you are doing and how to do it. In the pages that follow you will find a wealth of good advice that has helped other people to overcome nerves and become confident speakers.

1 Preliminaries

1 The good speaker

What makes a good speaker? We have no difficulty in judging the performance of others. As people come out of a meeting or social function there is always plenty of comment about the speaker: 'Wasn't he marvellous?', 'Didn't she speak well?', 'What a splendid talk!' or 'I was so bored', 'It was a dreadful evening', 'What a waste of time!'

We all register a general impression and have no doubt in our own minds about the success or failure of a speech, but what are we actually reacting to? What are the elements that come together to make us say, 'That was an excellent speech'?

The personality of the speaker must come high on the list. However interesting the material, it will only make its effect if we can respond to the person presenting it. There is no getting away from the fact that a public speaker is a performer just as much as an actor or singer is. This does not mean that when you speak in public you have to 'put on an act' in the bad sense of the phrase. It does mean that in presenting your talk you are also presenting yourself. Therefore voice, appearance and manner are all vital to your success as a speaker. This is not said in order to frighten off those already scared about speaking in public. It is simply common sense – and common experience, as anyone who has ever listened to a talk knows.

There is no need to be put off by this awareness of the importance of the speaker's own personality. On the contrary, it can give you confidence if you realize that nothing is more interesting to the audience than another person and that every one of us is unique. It is so common for a person to think that he or she is very ordinary and dull and has nothing of interest to share with others, yet there are few of us who do not have some special knowledge or experience – that certain something that makes us just a little bit different from everyone else. If you have been invited to speak in public, however humble the occasion, then somebody thinks you are interesting enough for other people to sit and listen to you. So away with false modesty! Be prepared to share your interests and reveal something of yourself in the process. An account of your trip to Africa in itself is a dead thing. It will only come to life when it is associated with your personality as presenter. If you are reticent and unforthcoming, the wonderful material you have will become tedious; if you allow your own enthusiasm to show through, the talk will be transformed.

The personality of the speaker is revealed in all sorts of ways, but there can be no doubt that the voice is the most important of all. Voices are quite fascinating; no two are exactly alike. They are capable of infinite variety, differing in tonal qualities, pitch and volume. Some people are endowed by nature with voices of strength and power, rich in resonance and satisfyingly musical in tone. But others have voices that are weak and breathy or harsh and monotonous, and unpleasing to listen to for any length of time. If you are dissatisfied with your vocal abilities yet are anxious to succeed as a speaker, you can take heart from the knowledge that voice training can effect great improvements; the section on voice later in this book will give you exercises that you can use to develop your vocal powers.

'Can you hear me at the back?' No public speaker should need to make this amateurish appeal. It is your job to be heard clearly in every part of the hall where you are speaking. If you can't, then you need to work harder on developing your voice and your diction. What audiences expect above all from a speaker is the ability to hear him clearly and without straining. In a very large hall, a microphone and a public address system are of the greatest assistance (providing you know how to use them properly), but it is astonishing how many intelligent and potentially interesting speakers doom themselves from the start by a failure to speak up. Such speakers – and there are very many of them – seem quite unable to put themselves in the place of the audience and assess their own audibility. They are also totally unaware of the vocal powers locked up inside them and waiting to get out. Just imagine the vibrant carrying power of the scream they would utter if approached by a madman with a knife. Yet the same vocal apparatus is used so meekly when they are making a speech that people in the third row can hardly hear a thing! So quality of voice and skill in using it stand very high in our list of what makes a successful speaker.

Personality shows itself in more ways than one. Voice is tremendously important, but there are other things that signal to the audience the sort of people we are. There is personal appearance – the way you are dressed and the care you have taken over your grooming. A great deal is conveyed by this, including that most important aspect, your opinion of the audience. If you have taken no trouble over your appearance, you are telling the audience indirectly that you do not think they matter very much. But you have to be sensitive to the situation: immaculate evening dress when you come to talk to teenagers in a youth club would hardly put you on terms with your listeners – unless of course your subject was ballroom dancing, in which case a sweater and jeans would not be very appropriate either.

Your stance, your mannerisms, your movements – controlled or fidgety – all convey something about your personality and will affect your success as a public speaker. A later chapter will consider all these in detail. But when all is said and done, you cannot succeed unless your material is good. You need to be very skilled indeed to please an audience with thin material. Perhaps a celebrity can do it, because audiences have come to see this famous person in the flesh, and are not too much concerned with what he or she has to say, provided they can tell their friends they have seen the face and heard the voice that usually comes from the television screen. But even with a celebrity, there will be a sense of disappointment if the subject-matter of the talk lacks real interest; a young lady who won a competition to visit a famous pop star remarked afterwards that she would have had a more interesting time if she had spent it at home with her husband.

If you have been invited to give a talk, you can assume that this is because the organizers have reason to believe you can interest their audience. It may be that your occupation is in the news at the time and they are hoping for information about it from the inside; perhaps your expertise in a craft or a hobby has reached their ears or they know you have been on an exciting trip or have done something unusual. Whatever the reason, the organizers have faith in your ability to interest and entertain their group. You can therefore take courage from this fact alone. It is then up to you to fulfil their expectations.

This will need careful thought, planning and rehearsal. You will find that the best speakers take the greatest care: they know the pitfalls. Of course with experience comes ease of delivery, the confidence to introduce variations to your prepared text and a readiness to improvise when something unforeseen happens. But none of these skills removes the necessity for careful preparation of your material in the first place, and that is why an important section of this book is devoted to planning your speech.

Having the right material, a serviceable voice and good general presentation, a speaker must still add something else to satisfy his audience and himself. This is sincerity. Whether you are making the most light-hearted speech, full of jokes and witticisms, or giving a profound discourse on the meaning of life itself, you must on no account merely spin words that mean nothing to you personally. An audience senses very quickly that this is happening and their attitude to speech and speaker deteriorates at once. An example of this is the political speech in which the speaker avoids the question and ignores the facts in order to maintain the party line, although we cannot think he really believes it himself.

To speak in public may appear daunting to a beginner, but it is also an exhilarating experience. If you are reading this book, it must be because you too feel you would like to respond to this challenge. It may be that someone has unexpectedly asked you to make a speech; on the other hand you may feel that you have something to offer to audiences and would like to acquire the skill to do so. Whatever the reason for your interest, you are showing an awareness – which is being increasingly acknowledged in our competitive world – that the ability to speak with confidence to a listening group is a source of personal power and fulfilment. The growth of the teaching of spoken English in schools and its central place in examinations shows that the world of education recognizes its importance. It is interesting that in an age increasingly dominated by computer technology, we are finding that the contact of person with person through the medium of speech is becoming more, rather than less, important; those who are skilled in its use have an enormous advantage in both social and professional affairs.

This book will help you to explore for yourself the many areas that make up what is known as public speaking – and they are far more numerous than the traditional after-dinner speech referred to at the beginning of the Introduction. After initial guidance, the best teacher is experience, and so you should take every opportunity that comes your way to practise the art of speaking in public. The first attempt may be nerve-racking, but imagine the thrill when someone comes up to you afterwards and says, 'I *did* enjoy your speech . . .'

2 Your nerves and you

George Bernard Shaw wanted to be a public speaker, yet he suffered dreadfully from nerves when he began his career. In characteristic fashion, GBS took steps to deal with the problem: he sought out a singer to teach him voice production and he accepted every invitation that came his way to speak in public. Many of his audiences were rough working men, in those days highly suspicious of the new socialist arguments that this eager young Irishman was putting to them. Heckling was intense but Shaw, nervous as he often was, persevered. From this baptism of fire emerged one of the finest public speakers of his time.

Few of us will be able to conquer our nerves by facing a hostile audience from a revolutionary platform. That really is doing it the hard way. But the experience of Bernard Shaw is relevant in showing us that nerves can and do affect almost everyone, even a man endowed, like Shaw, with a marvellous command of language. Every actor and musician knows the feeling of 'butterflies' before he goes on stage and many of the finest performers never lose it to the end of their careers. The great Russian bass, Chaliapin, was so nervous in one of his early performances that he backed towards a chair that wasn't there, tried to sit on it and ended up sprawled on the stage.

These tales of woe may not encourage you if you are already nervous at the very idea of speaking in public, but they do show that being nervous is very natural and extremely common, and that you are by no means alone in feeling worried about speaking. The chances are that nine out of ten people (and possibly ten out of ten) who enrol for a class in public speaking do so chiefly because they are scared. One such student remarked, 'The most terrifying moment of my life was the first time I had to stand up and make a speech in class.' Happily by the end of the course she was speaking confidently and effectively – which was just as well since by profession she was a lawyer.

It may help if we try to analyse just why we suffer from nerves when we have to appear before an audience. At the root is a very healthy feeling – a desire to please. But along with it comes that heart-stopping thought that, far from pleasing your audience, you are about to make a fool of yourself. All the long-developed image of our own adequacy which makes us able to survive in our work and our social life is suddenly placed at risk when we stand alone on a platform and everyone else turns to us with complete attention, waiting to assess us – our words, our appearance, our total personality. We are having to expose ourselves in an unfamiliar and – to us – an unnatural situation. The fact that the audience is almost certainly on our side, anxious for us to be successful (for that will give them pleasure also) is beside the point. As we see it, too much can go wrong: our voices may squeak, our notes become muddled, our arguments become confused and – worst of all – we may feel the attention of our audience slipping from us minute by minute until we hear the fatal rustling which indicates that general boredom has set in and that soon there will be a line of figures creeping towards the door.

Of course our fears grossly exaggerate the probable consequences, but that does not help us as we stand sweating in the wings or clutching our notes as the chairman goes through his introduction. So what should we do to get a grip on these nerves that can affect us long before we reach the platform and, indeed, may have given us sleepless nights for weeks?

The first thing is to accept that nerves are perfectly natural, that nearly every performer suffers from them to a greater or lesser degree, and that, paradoxically, they can be a help. The nerves are due to an injection of chemicals into the bloodstream to enable you to face a crisis. It is the same mechanism that gives a deer the extra energy to outrun its hunters. If you did not feel nerves, you would be an insensitive person and your performance would probably lack the zest that you would like to bring to it.

While it may be comforting to know this, it is not a good deal of help as you contemplate the dread task ahead of you or rise trembling to your feet. The chemicals that nature intended should assist you in running away from a problem prove a nuisance – the nervous symptoms cannot be worked off in running from the hall and diving into a taxi to take you away as far as possible from the audience who have come to hear you.

Somehow or other you have to control those nerves. Let's be honest: if you are a beginner, you are unlikely to succeed completely at your first attempt. Remember Bernard Shaw. He kept at it, facing turbulent audiences and no doubt disliking the experience intensely at first, but determined to overcome his fears because he desperately wanted to communicate his ideas to his fellow men. Therefore you have to accept that in order to control your nerves you have to pluck up courage, accept invitations and actually stand up and speak. Once you have done so successfully (and the chances are that after your first attempt you *will* have some reason to congratulate yourself), you will find that the second attempt holds less terror for you — and so on, as you gain experience and increasingly know what you are doing.

Knowing what you are doing is surely the key to the control of nerves. The speaker who has spent his time worrying rather than preparing his material, and planning and rehearsing his talk, is asking for trouble. But if you set out calmly to ensure that you know what you are going to say and how you are going to say it, then you will approach the event with an inner security that will already be putting those nerves in their place.

Your confidence will also be increased by finding out as much as you can in advance about the audience you will meet and the hall in which you will speak. One of the worst terrors is fear of the unknown, so make sure that you know as much as possible about the circumstances in which you will talk as well as about your own material.

Planning the hours before you speak is important. Leave yourself plenty of time to get ready. This will include a confidence-building final glance at your notes before you leave home and a check that you have put together all the things you need, which could be anything from a set of visual aids to a brush and comb. Nothing is more upsetting than finding you are falling behind your pre-performance schedule, and having to make a frantic dash to the hall, wondering if you have brought everything with you.

It really is important to arrive in good time. It sets the organizer's mind at rest and it helps your nerves by giving you time to become accustomed to the hall or room in which you are to speak. You will also be able to take the measure of the audience as they arrive or during the early part of the meeting. Almost certainly you will find that they are much less terrifying than you imagined and you will become aware that these people have come away from their firesides or gardens because they actually want to listen to you.

You may be worried that the audience is full of experts who know more about the subject than you do, but this is highly unlikely. You are the person who has been invited to speak and this must be because the organizers consider you to be the best person for the job. There may indeed be one or two people present who also have a good knowledge of your subject. Your nerves will tell you that these people are just sitting there waiting to catch you out, smiling to themselves at their superior knowledge and wondering how such an ignoramus could have been invited to address them. Of course your nerves have got it all wrong. People who already know the subject well will be among the most interested members of your audience; they will enjoy hearing their pet topic discussed and they will enliven the question-and-answer session with informed and intelligent contributions. Do not fear the possible expert in the audience: he is likely to be the most appreciative member present.

Nerves have an uncanny knack of hitting a person in the very place where he needs most control. If he is a pianist, his fingers are likely to feel stiff, if he is an athlete his legs will feel unsteady. And a speaker? Of course the nerves go straight to your vocal organs, the lungs and the larynx. Voice control depends on breath control, and one of the commonest symptoms of panic is rapid shallow breathing. Therefore tackle this enemy when he launches his attack, which will be just before you rise to speak. Take a number of slow deep breaths. You can start with a few deep breaths at home as you dress for the meeting and then, if you are given a room to yourself before you go on the platform, you can make yourself breathe slowly as you wait. Finally, in the short period when you are being introduced, two or three deep breaths will steady you just before you begin to speak. This will not only calm you emotionally; it will bring under control the breathing whose management is vital to the projection of your voice.

A simple relaxing exercise before you go on to the platform will also help. If you are alone for a few minutes, stretch your arms and hands up to their fullest extent and then slowly take the tension in turn out of the fingers, the hands, the wrists, the shoulders and so on until your whole body feels floppy and relaxed. If you are wearing formal clothes, you might need to modify this exercise somewhat, but even the act of simply tensing the arms and hands and then consciously letting the tension go from them is helpful. Gentle shoulder and head rolling is another exercise to remove the rigidity which your nerves are inducing in your body.

As for the voice, one or two of the simpler exercises given in Chapter 31, 'You and your voice', may be used. If you are likely to be amid your audience almost as soon as you enter the hall, you can do a few warming up exercises in your car as you drive to the meeting. If time and circumstances permit nothing more, then a few humming exercises to warm the voice and invoke some resonance are useful. If this does nothing else, it will at least convince you that you still have a voice and that it is ready at your service.

At last you begin your talk and, like someone who has just jumped from a diving board, you know there is no turning back. Your nerves will not leave you alone at this stage – it may be their last chance to wreak havoc before you discover that things are actually going rather well. They will mount another assault on your breathing muscles and your reaction will be to speak too quickly and at too high a pitch. But not if you are prepared! Knowing that rapid speech is a very common reaction to nerves, you should make a point of speaking firmly and slowly at the beginning of your talk. Your preliminary deep breathing should already have brought a measure of confidence; now build on it with a consciously controlled pace. This does not mean of course that you should begin with funereal slowness, but simply that you should pace your words rather more deliberately at first than might seem absolutely necessary. Once the initial contact with the audience is made and your nerves are in retreat, you can adopt the pace you have rehearsed and consider adequate for the size of the hall and the audience.

Similarly you should be conscious of the pitch of your voice. If excitement is causing you to speak on a higher note than usual, then you should deliberately lower the pitch, combining this with the slower speed already mentioned.

With experience you will come to recognize that nerves of some sort are simply part of the job, stimulating you to give of your best.

The really distressing kind can be overcome and they are likely to disappear as you become accustomed to public speaking and used to applying the advice given in this chapter. Most performers would feel that something was lacking if there was not that little flutter of 'butterflies' just before an appearance: it is part of the thrill of being on stage.

3 Your audience and you

Public speaking is all about communication and that involves a two-way traffic. If you concentrate all your thoughts on yourself and your speech, you are ignoring a vital half of the partnership – the audience. It may seem at first to be a many-headed monster waiting to devour you, but one of the joys of public speaking is winning a response from a group of people who have come for a variety of reasons to hear you. Nothing is more satisfying than the awareness that you have the rapt attention of an audience and are holding them in the palm of your hand. Such moments are rather special even for experienced speakers and they do not happen on every occasion; but when they do, the long hours of preparation, the nerves and the anxieties all seem worthwhile. You really have made contact.

When you are invited to speak, find out all you can about the audience. In some situations you may already know a great deal about them: this is especially true on family occasions. If you are to propose the toast of the bride and the groom at a wedding or make a farewell speech to a colleague who has worked with you for twenty years, unfamiliarity with the audience is unlikely to be your problem. The difficulty will be that you have to appear in an unaccustomed role. The family of the bride has various mental images of you as the good old friend of the family – an affectionate tolerance of the old boy and his peculiarities may be the predominant attitude of the younger generation. Suddenly he is to appear as a public speaker with everyone (for once!) paying attention to what he has to say – and this includes distant relatives, seen only on such occasions, and the inevitable nieces and nephews who are more interested in their first-ever glass of champagne than in what the speakers have to say. Here you have to operate the rule that applies whatever the audience – be sensitive and be yourself.

Sensitivity means being aware of the cross-currents of feelings and attitudes among your listeners. On a family occasion these are likely to be complex. The bride will not want to be embarrassed by the old friend of the family regaling the company with reminiscences of her childhood which she would rather forget. Visiting relatives may be offended if one set of cousins is mentioned and not another. Heavy emphasis on married bliss may be tactless if there are divorced people present. The speaker at a family occasion has to tread a very careful path and an unguarded aside can destroy the harmony of what was to be an enjoyable event.

If you follow the advice 'be yourself', you will avoid the worst fault of any public speaker – insincerity. A formal occasion will need your best manner, clearest voice and a well-prepared text, but it will certainly not require you to present yourself as something other than you are. If you are the sort of person who can never tell funny stories effectively and finds it difficult to make witty remarks, then do not set out to be a jester. Your laboriously gathered jokes will fall flat, the audience will shuffle with embarrassment and your own misery will be complete – and all because you are trying to present yourself as something other than you really are.

It is here that the role of the speaker, despite the many similarities, differs from that of the actor. The latter is trained to play many different characters and we admire his talent in appearing one day as a romantic lover and the next day as a blood-stained villain. It is something of a condemnation to say, as we do of some actors, that he always plays himself. We expect an actor during his career to play a large number of different people convincingly. But this is not the case for the public speaker. What an audience responds to is a sincere person doing his best to share his thoughts, knowledge and experience.

With sensitivity and sincerity as your watchwords, consider the audience you are to address. What you do not already know you will need to find out from the organizers of the event. The size of the audience is of course important: it may determine the style of your talk, the kind of visual aids you can employ and the degree of formality that will be appropriate. If you are to speak to a dozen or so people, your approach will be quite different from that which you adopt when you speak to an audience of two hundred. With a small group, your presentation may become a friendly talk with a high degree of informality, whereas the large audience will demand a much more structured approach.

Yet even this cannot be taken for granted. You need to know who the people in the audience are and the nature of the organization that has brought them together. If the occasion is right for it, a really skilled speaker can make a hundred people feel like one happy family, while the presentation of an important business topic to six executives may require very great care and formality to match the seriousness of the meeting and the importance of those present.

Consider also what points of contact you are likely to have with your audience. There is all the difference in the world in being asked to talk to the local philatelic society about your collection of Middle Eastern stamps and being asked to address a luncheon club fifty miles from your home town on the same subject. In the first instance, the points of contact are already well established. Both you and the audience are interested in stamps and know a good deal about them. You speak the same language: technical terms and stamp-collectors' jargon can be used freely with no necessity for you to explain or re-phrase for the uninitiated. You can rely on your audience's interest in your topic, though it will be up to you to maintain and increase it by the quality of your talk. The questions afterwards will be challenging and well informed, and you will be on your metal to satisfy the audience that you are the expert they assume you to be. But you will be at ease in the knowledge that, as far as your hobby goes, these people are your own kind and speak the same language.

The luncheon club fifty miles away is a different proposition. You have been asked to speak to them on the same topic – postage stamps of the Middle East, but who is this audience and why have they invited you? You discover that members of this club meet monthly to enjoy a meal together and to listen to a variety of topics that their committee believe will interest them. Someone has told them about your stamp collection and so you have been invited to be their guest speaker. Points of contact are not entirely lacking, but they are fewer than with the local philatelic society and this will necessitate a complete rewriting of your talk. The chief point of contact is that these are open-minded people who are prepared to be interested in a wide range of topics and have reason to believe that you can speak entertainingly to them for thirty minutes or so. You may think that there can be no further points of contact, but brief reflection will remind you that everyone knows something about postage stamps –

if only how to stick them on envelopes – and, more seriously, very many people have had stamp collections when they were children and probably regret that they abandoned the hobby in their youth. Current news items from the Middle East may give you another point of contact, as may the perennial interest we all have in the things other people collect. Suddenly you realize that this audience of strangers with no knowledge of philately is a group with whom you can make contact in several ways.

Naturally your approach to a group of philatelists will not do here. There is likely to be far less interest in water marks, perforations and errors of printing, and far more on the development of postal services in far-away places, the pictorial aspect of the stamps and the reasons why you yourself became a collector. You cannot use the technical jargon which you could take for granted with your fellow philatelists. The talk may have the same title, but what you say to the luncheon-club audience will be very different.

Follow this technique with all the audiences you are called on to address. Find out the points of contact and frame your speech to include them. Then, having established links, you will be able to branch out and introduce the audience to aspects of your subject which are new to them and they will go away with the satisfied feeling that they have really learnt something from you.

The motives that bring an audience together to hear a talk are bound to be mixed. Some members will have come out of genuine interest in what you have to say; others will come because they regularly attend the meetings, whatever the topic for the evening. A certain number will come a little reluctantly, in response to a pressing invitation from the organizer or another member anxious to build up the audience to a respectable size. Some will be present because friends have brought them and a few may be there because their lives are lonely and an event such as your speech will take them out of their homes and into the company of others. Of course you cannot take account of all these different motives, but it is as well to remember that an audience is made up of individuals and some strange chemistry welds them together into a single body with a character of its own. One main ingredient in the chemistry is you, the speaker. You will be the one responsible for the audience leaving the hall either pleased and stimulated or bored and dispirited.

Most audiences hope for two things from the speaker – to be interested and to be entertained. The balance of these two elements will vary with the circumstances: the element of entertaining in briefing a group of colleagues about a new project which your firm is undertaking is not likely to be high, whereas the interest should be considerable. However, even in the most serious and businesslike presentation, a modicum of entertainment is not to be despised. If you want to gain the cooperation and sympathetic attention of fellow businessmen, there is nothing wrong with lightness of touch in your introduction and some humorous relief at carefully judged points along the way.

In other situations the audience will be hoping for quite a substantial element of entertainment. Social occasions by their very nature are meant to put people into a good humour and so after-dinner speeches, proposing toasts at business and family events are a time for a lighthearted approach. But some entertainment is also expected from a speaker invited to address such groups as Women's Institutes, luncheon clubs and 'over sixties'. New interest and information is looked for, but so is the pleasing feeling that one is being entertained by a visitor with an attractive manner, an agreeable voice and a sense of humour.

It is also a good idea to try and find out why you and your subject have been chosen. In probing this, you may discover that the group you are to address has a very particular interest in your topic. Perhaps they are to feature various aspects of it in their season's programmes; perhaps it is one facet of a more general subject they wish to explore. This sort of information will almost certainly affect the way you will present your topic. You may even be told by the organizer the aspect he would like you to develop. None of this information should be disregarded. A sensitive response to local requirements will pay handsome dividends in audience response.

This does not mean that a well-prepared talk can only be used on one occasion. Of course it can be presented successfully to several different audiences, but only if they are roughly of the same kind. If the audience differs markedly in any way from the ones for whom you have prepared the speech, then you must be ready to recast it. In fact every audience is different and some small modifications may be needed every time you give it. What is more, you are likely to find after one presentation that certain parts of the speech have not gone as well as others. These are the ones you will want to revise and rewrite before you offer them to another audience.

4 Getting the facts right

One of the important preliminaries in preparing a speech is to reinforce your personal knowledge with background research. Even within our special subject, none of us can really know everything, though we may know a great deal more than most. As we set about planning what we are going to say, we gradually become aware of gaps in our knowledge. An uneasy feeling creeps in that perhaps we may not know as much as we thought we did. Questions may be put to us on aspects about which we are a little hazy; a vital link is missing in a chain of details which we hoped to present. We are just not sure of all the facts and this is something that must be put right. An audience has the right to expect that the speaker will not get his facts wrong. Background research is essential.

The need for this is also likely to arise if your involvement with the subject has been personal and vivid but limited to a single experience. A travel talk would be a good example of this. Your holiday on a canal in the south of France was full of incident; it took you to strange and fascinating places and provided you with excellent material for a talk. But as you order this material and try and shape it into a speech, you realize that you need to know something about the construction of this canal; you also feel that some historical background will be necessary when you describe the attractions of the ancient towns you passed through on your leisurely journey. Perhaps you attended a folk festival (of which you have attractive slides), but you now think your audience will want a fuller explanation of what was going on than you can provide on the basis of what you saw on that single day last August. You are going to have to find out more.

The Library

The best resource for fact finding is the public library. Even if you are completely inexperienced in using a library, you need have no fear. Simply explain to the librarian what you want to know

and he or she will be of the greatest assistance. However, it is far
better to develop some personal skills in finding out information for
yourself. Make yourself acquainted with the classification system of
your local library (the chances are that it will be the widely used
Dewey Decimal System); the librarian will be helpful here. Then be
prepared to use the catalogues, which will be in the form of card-
indexes or microfiches.

It is best to start with the subject-index. This will give you the
classification numbers under which you will find the books relevant
to your subject. The topic you are researching may stray across a
number of subject boundaries, which means that the books will be
shelved in different parts of the library, possibly in unexpected
places. For example, if you are researching 'Pollution', you will find
no less than ten different catalogue numbers in the standard Dewey
subject-index, including pollution of the air and of water, industrial
pollution and the sociological aspects.

Once you have discovered from the subject-index which sections
of the library are of interest to you, you may be tempted to take the
short cut of going straight to the shelves to see what you can find.
But this could be inefficient; books may be out on loan; in a big
library older books may be stacked elsewhere, and obtainable only
on request. By going directly to the open shelves you overlook these
possibilities. It is far better to go from the subject-index to the general
classified catalogue, where all the books are listed in subject sections, and there look up the reference numbers given in the subject
catalogue. In this way you obtain a complete list of all the books the
library contains on your subject. At this point you can write down
the titles which you think will be of particular interest to you and
then seek them on the shelves. If they are not there, you can ask the
librarian about them. If they are out on loan they can be reserved for
you when they are returned. If they are in a basement stack, the
librarian will fetch them for you.

The public library service in the UK is extensive and efficient. If
your library does not contain a book that you want, it can be obtained
for you through the inter-library service which links libraries in all
parts of the country. Of course such orders take time, but your local
librarian will be able to advise you about this.

Most libraries have reference sections, with books that are available for consultation in the library only. If you have access to a library in a big town or city, you will find that it contains a large and well-stocked reference department with desks for private study. This is the happy hunting ground for researchers – and that certainly includes public speakers gathering material for their talks.

Here you will find the great encyclopaedias which can quickly solve so many of our research problems. Some, like the *Encyclopaedia Britannica*, may run to thirty volumes or more. Others pack their information into one volume. Whatever kind you use, the same basic principle applies: use the *index* before you go searching for the alphabetical entry. The index of an encyclopaedia will refer you to the main entry on your subject and, possibly, to several other entries where it is also referred to. It may be that the very information you are looking for is contained in one of these subsidiary references and you would have missed it completely if you had looked up only the main alphabetical entry.

There are a number of standard reference books that will give you facts and figures. These include *Whitaker's Almanack* and *The Statesman's Year-Book*. For biographical matter you can consult the *Dictionary of National Biography* if you are researching a historical figure, and the various annual publications such as *Who's Who* for people who are still living. In the arts, the series of Oxford Companions (to literature, art, music, theatre, etc.) is invaluable.

You will probably find that the reference library has specialist books on your own subject as well as a wide range of general reference books.

Specialist organizations

There is another source of information that can be easily overlooked, namely the numerous organizations that exist to foster special interests. These range from such widely known organizations as the National Trust and the Royal Geographical Society, to smaller groups of enthusiasts whose interests cover most things from the study of Sherlock Homes to the playing of tiddly-winks. (Yes, such an organization *does* exist.) Once again your local librarian should be able to produce a list of all such bodies with the addresses of their secretaries. You may well find that a letter to the appropriate organization will elicit the information you are looking for or at any rate advice on where to find it. Very often these societies publish journals and maintain their own libraries, with valuable archives, containing far more specialized information than you could expect to find in a public library.

You may feel that a certain commercial firm can supply you with the information you need for your talk. Often such concerns are very helpful, but it is as well to remember that they are in business to manufacture goods or provide services, and not to write your talk for you. It costs them time and money to reply to you; so be modest in your requests, making clear exactly what you want to know – and enclose a stamped addressed envelope for reply.

Interviews

For some talks the most likely source of information will be other people. For example, you may be planning a talk on the history of your town. Nothing will be more fascinating than the reminiscences of older citizens who remember the place from their childhood and can recall stories told to them by their parents and grandparents, giving you a living contact with your subject over a span of eighty years or more. If your talk is to do with the future of your community, rather than its past, you may need to talk to local businessmen, administrators or council officials. If your subject is to do with education, you may need to canvass the opinions of parents, teachers and pupils.

In every case we can assume that you are already knowledgeable to some degree on your subject. But the need to reinforce this knowledge and bring it right up to date means that talking to others in the field will be an important part of your planning.

For a successful interview, you need to prepare carefully. Begin by asking yourself what you are hoping to discover; then frame a series of specific questions you would like to put to your interviewee to elicit this information or opinion. When you know what you want to ask, approach your expert, preferably by letter, asking for an interview and stating the reason why you wish for a talk. When you are given an appointment, be sure to arrive in good time, since you are already indebted to the person who is giving up time to you. You may want to take notes or even tape-record the interview. You must handle this with the greatest tact. Some people will shut up completely if they see a notebook flourished before them and a tape-recorder may frighten them out of their wits. It is better to keep notebook and recorder out of sight until you are sure that they will not give offence. Then the suggestion that you would like to write down that important piece of information – or even record it on tape – could be gently mooted. But it is better by far to rely on your memory until you have finished the interview than to ruin everything by an unguarded grab at your notebook.

The important thing is to create an atmosphere in which your interviewee will feel inclined to talk freely and easily. Your prepared list of questions are in your mind only as an aid to you in guiding the conversation the way you want it to go. But your man may want to take it his way and this may turn out to be even more rewarding than what you had in mind. If the interview is not yielding what you want to know, then you have to look out for moments in the course of the conversation when you can elicit the information indirectly, perhaps by picking up some apparently unrelated remark and steering it towards your goal.

Interviewing is an art and you must be prepared to adjust to persons and circumstances. A busy manager will appreciate directness and efficiency in your questions, while an elderly pensioner may enjoy the opportunity of a long and leisurely chat about memories which most people have not got time to listen to. Very often it is the casual remark or the unexpected reply that will open the door to something of considerable interest to you. Your prepared questions will be disregarded and material you never thought of will be offered. Be prepared for this kind of happy accident and do not brush it aside in pursuit of your own set questions.

One important point to clear up before you leave the interview is to find out whether you have permission to quote your interviewee by name in your speech. Some people will not wish to be quoted verbatim at all; others will not object if you say, for instance, 'a bank manager told me . . .' but do not use their name. It is essential that you play fair with somebody who has agreed to help you. If you are told something in confidence or off the record, you must respect this completely.

From all these sources – libraries, specialist organizations, personal interviews – you build up your own background of knowledge, giving yourself the ability to speak confidently on your subject because you really do know a great deal about it. On the platform, you are the person in authority. The audience does not expect you to know absolutely everything about your topic, but it will be disappointed if your knowledge is shown to be sketchy and superficial. Researching the background will always be worthwhile – and it's fun finding out!

2 Planning a Talk

5 Gathering material

The telephone rings. You answer it nonchalantly, without a care in the world. A voice at the other end identifies itself, makes the usual polite noises and then says (after the pause which indicates that the small talk is over and the point of the conversation has arrived), 'We understand you have just returned from Borneo. We would very much like you to come and talk to our luncheon club about it. What about the second Thursday of the month after next?'

From that very moment your preparations for giving the talk begin. You may not realize it at the time: you will be too busy feeling flattered and flustered — looking at your diary, pencilling in the date, agreeing to all the arrangements that the pleasant voice on the phone is explaining, and thinking how pleased your wife or husband will be to hear that you have been invited. There may even be a fee, larger than you would have expected. All these delightful things will fill your mind for at least two minutes. After that comes the dreadful thought, 'What am I going to say? I've never done anything like this before.'

Actually one corner of your mind began working on this the instant your caller invited you to speak. You make a rapid mental assessment of your knowledge of the subject and your own capabilities. You realized that your experiences in Borneo were potentially full of interest to others and that you were sufficiently intelligent to put some of them into words. So you said yes to the invitation and now you are in for it!

The engagement is roughly two months away and so you tell yourself there is no need for panic. You will have to think about it next month and then really get down to it. With that happy thought you resume your normal way of life, indulging the pleasant pursuit of dropping into casual conversations the fact that you have received an invitation to address the prestigious luncheon club and that although you have never done this sort of thing before, you really are rather looking forward to it. You may detect among the admiring looks you receive a disturbing suggestion that your friends are think-ing 'Rather you than me', and it does cross your mind that quite a lot of work lies ahead if you are not to make a complete fool of yourself and that you had better do something about it next week rather than next month.

You have therefore learnt the first lesson in preparing a speech: let your mind begin working on it as soon as possible. In fact some of your mind will already have begun work. You will find that in odd moments thoughts about Borneo will occur to you and you will say to yourself, 'Oh, I must remember to mention that in my talk.' The germinating of such seeds in your mind is a valuable part of the process of preparation and, unless the speech is scheduled for the very near future, it is probably a good thing to give the mind a few days to take on board the idea that you will in due course have to give a talk. You will find that thoughts and memories, useful in the speech, come to mind, and ideas of what you may want to say begin to crystallize.

Soon, however, you have to become purposeful and businesslike. There is an important job to be done and it is going to take longer than you thought. Therefore you will have to sit down at your desk and make a start. The time factor is important. Preparing a speech is a time-consuming activity and any thought that you only need a few short notes to unlock the stream of reminiscences that will flow in abundance once you stand up is a recipe for disaster. The most careful planning, writing and rehearsal are needed in order to pro-duce the apparently spontaneous and entertaining talk your listeners are hoping for. So no short cuts and no leaving things to the last moment!

The first thing to do when you sit down with the dauntingly blank piece of paper in front of you is to jot down straight away the first thoughts that come into your head about Borneo (or whatever your chosen subject is). They need have no connection with each other. Your first might be 'I loved my bungalow by the sea', and the second might be 'The population of Borneo is about six million.' These are two unrelated facts. It does not matter. Just keep writing for as long as you can.

In theory your paper will soon be covered on both sides with masses of closely written jottings, all splendid material for your talk. Common experience, however, warns us that in practice your string of ideas may peter out before you have written a third of a page and this may happen even more quickly with a subject less immediately personal than recent experiences in the Far East.

The list of jottings is the raw material of your talk and it is therefore important that you make it as substantial as you can. If you really cannot produce more than four or five random jottings, then you must face the possibility that you have chosen the wrong subject. However, there are techniques to help you to build up the fund of material which is almost certainly locked away in your mind if the subject has any significance for you at all. How can you unlock this hoard?

Once the first flow of jottings dries up, go back over each idea in turn and challenge it to produce one more idea for you by free association. For example, that point about your bungalow by the sea should be productive. The word 'sea' by itself might produce all sorts of thoughts and memories: travelling to the island by sea; sea-borne trade; fishing – and *that* word reminds you of a memorable day when the islanders took you fishing in their boat; the boat – that could be another idea, leading to a description of how such vessels are made and that could take you on to local crafts in general. From this might come thoughts about the economy of the island and then government policy, which would remind you of the important people in the part of the island you visited, some of whom you met personally. All this flow of material came from the one word 'sea'!

Let us take a more abstract title and assume that someone has asked you to give a talk on the English language, perhaps under the title 'The English We Speak Today'. We may assume that you would not have accepted this engagement if you did not have some interest in and, we may hope, a little specialized knowledge of the subject. All the same, you do not need to be a profound scholar of linguistics to put together an agreeable and thought-provoking talk on your own language. Yet, compared with a subject such as Borneo, the topic is more demanding because the material is more diffuse and less pictorially vivid.

Your first ideas to be jotted down might be something like this: variety of accents; the pop scene; influence on language of immigrant groups; sloppy speech of the young; speech as a feature of class identity. If you paused at this point and wondered what to write down next, you could take up 'pop scene' and see what associations it would suggest. Rapidly you would find yourself writing: pop scene; teenagers and language; new words and slang; language used to exclude older generation; pop and the media. This could lead to the influence of the media on language. The list begins to grow. That jotting about the contribution to English of immigrant groups would quickly lead to thoughts about English as an international language and the effect of this on the development of English in the twentieth century. (As an exercise, see if you can lengthen this list of notes on 'The Language We Speak', using the free association method to add new ideas. Then you could choose topics of your own and practise developing lists of basic material in this way.)

There are other methods of assembling material, in addition to the free association method just described. If your subject is not entirely abstract – and very few subjects are – then when you think of the topic, *pictures* must flit in and out of your mind. A geographic topic (such as our old friend Borneo) is obviously very visual indeed, but there is surely a visual element in titles as varied as 'Street Crime in Our Century'; 'Lace-making'; 'The History of Chichester'; 'Bringing Up a Handicapped Child'; 'Building Your Own Aeroplane'; 'Touring Europe with a Guitar'; 'Famous Gardens'.

In each example there is so much to see – and not only to see, but also to hear and perhaps to touch and smell. Therefore bring your senses into play and use them to suggest material. If you take yourself on a mental tour of Chichester, you, the expert, will see things in your mind's eye that others would not notice and which will be a valuable addition to your talk. 'Seeing' a street crime will suggest a number of important details about time and place, attitudes and reactions that will be more vivid and stimulating for your audience than a string of statistics put together from a Home Office report.

Reminding yourself of the sense of hearing will also pay dividends in the search for ideas. The sounds made by a handicapped child will remind you of his or her problems with communication; the sound of your aeroplane may suggest something about the tuning of the engine and the very absence of sound in a certain famous garden may yield you a valuable talking-point about the beauty of silence and the desecration of another garden by the roar of traffic from a nearby motorway.

The delicacy of touch necessary in lace-making; the fingers made raw by too much playing for one's supper on that guitar in Europe; the texture of old stones in a historic town: these are three examples where the sense of touch can produce points for your growing list. You can try for yourself to find ideas useful in talks on these subjects from the sense of smell!

As you consider how you can add to your store of material, bring the word 'people' into your mind. Think of people engaged in the activity you want to talk about and ask yourself what they are doing and why. Not only will more ideas occur to you, but you will be providing yourself with a most valuable feature of your talk. Audiences love to hear about the real people involved in your subject. Even something as technical as 'Building Your Own Aeroplane' will be all the better for those moments when you are able to talk about the people who helped you, the special skills this one brought to the project and the sense of humour contributed by another during a difficult time. With 'Lace-making', a description of some of the makers in Honiton, and their background and achievements, will stimulate the audience and enliven your talk, while details of the gardeners who created your 'Famous Gardens' will add an extra dimension to your talk. 'Human' interest is a well-worn phrase, but it never ceases to be important.

Arguing a case

If your speech is intended to persuade or influence opinion, then there will have to be some modification of the methods for gathering material just described. A political speech pressing for a certain line of action or a speech to a public meeting for or against some proposal that is arousing controversy in the community must be well argued and based on substantial points. You may feel passionately about the subject, but your speech will be ineffective if you have not clarified your own thinking and selected the points that are really going to tell.

You cannot do this until you have got out of your system all the multitude of thoughts and feelings that have stirred you. Get them down on paper in the form of jottings and include the little points as well as the big ones, the strong feelings (which your opponents will call your prejudices) as well as the calculated arguments. Only when all these are before you will you be able to consider objectively which are going to be the really telling points and which, you will have to admit, are weakly based. If you are surprised at how few things you have written down and yet you still feel passionately about the cause, this may be because there are only one or two basic points of principle on which everything turns. Yet these are not going to give you a speech of the length you want.

Use the technique, described in the previous section, of thinking of *people*. If your topic is to do with housing policy, call to mind as many examples as you can of people known to you who are suffering under existing conditions. What are their specific difficulties? This may remind you of an important effect of the policy which you had previously overlooked. Thinking of people will also provide you with much needed examples of the results of the policy you are attacking. Every political speaker knows that strings of statistics leave audiences bemused and distrustful, but a vivid description of the effects of a policy on individual cases can sway the audience by arousing their human sympathies. This technique of using one's five senses can also be of use here; the sights, sounds and smells of poor housing will enable the speaker to talk graphically of his concern about the way some people have to live.

Letting your ideas simmer

When you have had a session of hard and purposeful thinking about what you want to say in your talk and have jotted down as many as possible of these ideas, it will be as well to leave things for a couple of days. It is quite extraordinary how the mind will go on working at the problem without your being aware of it. Quite suddenly a new idea will present itself, or an extension of something already on your list. If the idea looks in any way promising, make a point of writing it down as soon as you can. Ideas can float away as easily as they come to the surface!

Not only will new ideas occur to you; the mind may begin to suggest a way of approaching the subject as a whole or it may throw up what seems a splendid opening remark. All this is to be welcomed. Your mind is jumping ahead to the next stage of your planning. It shows that your own interest in now fully engaged and there is every reason for you to return to your desk and begin to put these ideas into some sort of shape. You have the bricks; now you must begin to build the house.

6 What's your angle?

There is one more important decision to make before you can use your jottings as the basis for your talk: what line are you going to take? There are various ways of expressing this. Journalists sometimes speak of getting an angle on a story. Others talk of the approach, or the slant. But whatever you call it, it amounts to the same thing – your attitude to the subject and how you wish to present it to the audience. First of all you have to question your intentions in making the speech. Are you primarily interested in entertaining the audience, informing them, educating them, persuading them or moving them? Many speeches will include more than one of these elements and entertainment of some sort is inherent in a large number of speeches of all kinds; but it is very important to know your own motives in making a speech. It is equally important to consider what the organizers of the occasion are expecting from you. If you are not sure of this, then you should find out in discussion, preferably when the booking arrangements are being made. If you are invited to talk about Switzerland to a youth group because they are going on holiday there, you will concentrate on the scenery and the facilities for sport and entertainment in the area they plan to visit. You will not, one hopes, bore them with a long discourse on Swiss trade and the country's importance in international banking. If a music club invites you to talk on opera, your speech will be serious and scholarly because you will be talking to a knowledgeable audience. On the other hand, if a dining club makes you their guest, your talk on opera might concentrate on backstage stories and such operatic disasters as the tenor who swallowed his moustache at Covent Garden or the soprano who bounced back after her suicide leap over the battlements in *Tosca*!

It all depends on the line of approach or 'angle' which you think is right for you and your audience. Very often this means selecting from a number of options, any one of which might be suitable for this particular audience. Your subject is a famous historical figure, a statesman or general. You might concentrate on the biographical details such as his career, his love-affairs, and his marriage and family. On the other hand you might decide to treat all this very briefly, and concentrate on his contribution to history or on the development of his political thinking. If the man's life were very long and filled with many activities, you might wish to concentrate on one notable period only, there being insufficient time to treat the whole biography in considerable detail. Time is certainly a factor in this decision. One promising angle might need at least two hours to develop satasfactorily and this would have to be rejected if you only had forty-five minutes at your disposal.

Once you have chosen your line of approach, you must make sure you stick to it. A travel talk concentrating on the natural beauty of a particular country with its flora and fauna would be thrown off course if the speaker suddenly inserted a section on its internal politics and then, equally suddenly, returned to a description of the landscape. Similarly unsatisfactory would be the intrusion of gossipy personal anecdotes into the serious study of a period of history. The audience would become confused at the intentions of the speaker and uncertain about his motives in giving the talk.

7 Shaping the talk

You have now gathered in note form a useful body of material and you have decided on your line of approach. The time has arrived when you must turn these things into a talk.

The first step is to select from your jottings the items that relate to your chosen line of approach and ruthlessly delete those that are irrelevant to it. When you have done this, bring together those ideas that are closely related. For example, you may have noted down on one page a strong point in support of your argument and, on the next page, another point which reinforces the first one, together with two instances which would serve well as illustrations. Make a revised version of your jottings, rearranging the material from your original notes and bringing together ideas which are closely related. You now have before you the basic material for your talk, although other points will occur to you as the planning and writing proceed. You are approaching the moment when you can put pen to paper and write the first draft.

Before you do so, consider one further matter – the shape of your talk. It is a truism that every speech or piece of writing must have a beginning, a middle and an end. This may sound obvious but it is not always well followed in practice. What it really means is that you must care about the design of your talk, consciously shaping it so that the speech opens well, proceeds by clear stages to a well-placed climax and then is brought to a satisfying conclusion. The opening is so important that you may decide to write it *after* you have completed the main body of the speech. This may sound strange advice but it makes sense. When the speech has been completed, you will know exactly what you are going to say, the tone you are adopting and the effect you are hoping to achieve. You are therefore in a very good position to judge what kind of opening will best suit this particular talk. To start yourself off, you may well draft a possible opening straight away, but with the promise to yourself that you will go back to it later on and very possibly recast it completely. (See the next chapter, p. 48.)

There are so many different kinds of talks that detailed advice on internal structure is impossible to give. But there are some general points that are worth remembering in nearly all situations. First of all, make clear to your audience very early on what exactly your subject is and how you propose to treat it. Your talk may have a title that is rather vague and generalized. It may have been chosen to arouse curiosity rather than to impart detailed information. 'Days in the Sun' sounds attractive and may pull in an audience wearied by a prolonged winter, but it does not say much about the content of your speech, which could be anything from a holiday in the Caribbean to how to build your own summerhouse! Nor do 'Gardens I Have Known', 'Be Your Own Mechanic', or 'A Victorian Recipe Book'. Each of these titles gives some idea of the content of the talk, enough to bring people to the meeting (or keep them at home!), but once the talk begins the audience likes to know much more clearly what they are being offered. You should therefore clarify what you propose to talk about. This may become obvious from your opening remarks, but if this is not so, then your next task must be to set forth precisely what your subject is and the limits within which you intend to treat it. This need not be done formally or mechanically; it should appear as an integral part of your talk, presented easily and graciously, and quite briefly. When it is done, the audience should know what they are to expect. This is reassuring for them and they can adjust their own thinking so that it is in line with your approach. If you leave an audience with only a hazy idea of what is to come they will be ill at ease and may be irked as the speech develops in a way they are not prepared for.

Within the body of the speech, you should move forward by stages which are clear both to yourself and the audience. It is the equivalent of paragraphing in writing. Select from your revised list of jottings the point you want to make first and then the order in which you will take the others, pinpointing the highlights and shaping them all into a satisfying whole.

If you are presenting an argument and you have, say, four really good points to put forward, use your judgement to decide which one is your ace and reserve this for the climax of the talk. It is the point you will leave most firmly in the minds of your listeners when you sit down. Then select the one that will gain attention and sympathy for your cause at the start and make this your first point. The other two points will fall into place between the two principal ones. With a striking opening and a firm conclusion, your talk now has shape.

Other subjects will suggest their own pattern, though you must be aware of it and consciously use it in your planning. A talk on someone's life might start with childhood and continue with schooldays, career, retirement and death. An account of a holiday or of travels might follow the order of events – arrival, first days, highlights, return home. The history of a town or country would similarly suggest its own structure, based on chronological periods. The demonstration of a craft would move from a description of tools and materials, through the initial preparations, to the various stages of making, and would end with some comments on the final product.

In all these examples, the shape of the talk is inherent in the subject itself. For other speeches you will have to devise your own structure on the basis of your preliminary jottings. Certain guidelines will already be available. If you are proposing a toast at a wedding, you know that the climax will be when you invite the company to raise their glasses and drink to the happy couple. You know too that your opening is going to express your sense of the honour done you, as an old friend of the family, in being invited to propose the toast. As this kind of speech is best if it is kept brief, the arranging of the two or three gracious things you wish to say should not be difficult.

If you are giving a talk to a group of overseas visitors on, say, the educational provision in this country, you have the areas of primary, secondary and tertiary education as guide-posts to your structure. You will find that most talks suggest a structure to you when you sit down to plan the talk. The great thing is to be aware of the need for a shape to your speech and to ensure that it is clearly marked.

With all this in your mind and the revised list of jottings before you, the next step is to write a clear outline of your speech in note form. This is the plan from which you will write the full version of your speech. If the topic is 'The History of No-Town' such a plan might look like this:

> Opening – Anglo-Saxon settlement – how the monastery was built – effects of the Norman invasion – the import-

ance of trade in the Middle Ages – the dissolution of the monastery and the building of the manor house – what the Industrial Revolution meant to the town – the great fire and the destruction of the main street – nineteenth-century developments – No-Town and the two World Wars – its role in our own time – conclusion.

Such an outline is extremely useful in allowing you to survey the matter of the speech before you begin to write. It gives you the opportunity to prune material that you can already see is going to overload the speech. You can identify your climax points and decide where you are going to be more expansive in your talk and what you are going to deal with more briefly. A plan will also prevent you from digressing or losing track when you begin to write. It is up to you how much detail you put in your plan. If you wish, you can add supporting details and examples to the main headings. This is not time wasted. On the contrary, it can save time when you come to write the full version, because all the material is to hand.

Before you actually sit down to write your speech, it is a good idea to give some thought to language and style, and to your opening and conclusion. This is the subject of the next chapter.

8 Writing the talk

You are now about to write the speech. That sounds like a contradiction in terms. If you are *writing* English, you are using one mode of expression and if you are *speaking* English you are using a different one. You may be an excellent writer but there is no guarantee that you will be a good public speaker and, conversely, a first-rate speaker is by no means certain to be an effective writer. To complicate matters even further, you must remember that there are many different forms of spoken English. Just consider the speech used around a family breakfast table (assuming people are awake enough to want to say anything beyond 'Pass the marmalade') and compare it with that used in an office during a working day. Think of all the subtle changes one makes when speaking to the boss rather than to a junior colleague. Think too how your spoken language changes when you meet friends in a pub, and the different forms of speech you would use if you had to visit a solicitor on a matter of business or if you called on the vicar to arrange a wedding or christening.

To convey these many varieties of spoken English in writing requires the talents of a professional novelist or dramatist; merely to write as you speak is no recipe for successful writing. When a novel is adapted for the theatre it is sometimes found that the dialogue does not sit easily on the lips of the actors; it requires the special skills of a playwright to make stage speech seem realistic.

This shows how difficult it is to convey spoken English in writing. Yet when making a public speech, you need to prepare what you are going to say in *written* form, since it is only in this way that you can sit back and assess your material, and the shape and timing of the speech. As you write out your speech, however, you must think of it as *spoken English*, words which you yourself will be speaking to the audience, and not as a literary composition. The dullest speech is the one that sounds like a spoken essay. Artificial turns of phrase, faithful obedience to the rules of grammar and syntax (e.g. never end a sentence with a preposition; do not split infinitives), and finely honed prose have their place in written work, but tend to sound stilted and unnatural in speech.

Try to hear your own voice speaking aloud as you write. If it does not sound like you, then try again. Read a paragraph aloud when you have written it and decide whether it sounds convincing *as speech.* Use the normal contractions of speech — 'aren't', 'don't', 'isn't', 'haven't', 'I'd', 'won't', etc. Include the conversational phrases with which we seek the agreement of our listeners — 'aren't we?', 'don't we?', 'isn't it?' These are the normal currency of speech and should be made use of, even though they would appear much less frequently, if at all, in formal writing.

An example of a written text intended for speech is the radio or television news bulletin. The newsreaders' scripts are carefully written for them and are models of clarity and conciseness. On the other hand, ordinary citizens who come into the studio for an interview have no script — what they say is impromptu and has the spontaneity of real speech. Any attempt to write out an interview would be self-defeating.

As a public speaker you have to achieve a similar liveliness, but because your talk is to be far longer than an interview and you have no professional to feed you with questions, you have to start from a written script — but it must be a written script conceived as speech. Some experienced speakers make sure of this by writing only *outlines* of their talks, thereby forcing themselves to improvise the text when they are on their feet. The result is bound to be natural speech. But to use this method requires a great deal of confidence, much experience and complete certainty about one's own fluency. Such a speaker will be absolutely sure that he has a large vocabulary and a ready availability of speech structures so that, quite literally, he will never be at a loss for a word. It is not a method to be recommended to the inexperienced, who might well be overwhelmed by hesitations and stumblings if he tried it. It should remain as a possibility to be considered for the years ahead when you have proved yourself before audiences again and again. Even then, you will not necessarily want to try this method, but some will find it right for them and it does ensure the authentic sound of spoken English — the aim of everyone who speaks in public, whether he writes his speeches out or not.

With so many modes of spoken English to choose from, the beginner may well ask how he is to select the right one for his talk. This will depend on several factors: type and size of audience, the place where he is to speak, the nature of the occasion, the material of the talk and the personality of the speaker.

It is essential for the speaker to be himself. That is to say, his speech must sound quite natural to him, though within limits acceptable to his listeners. If the audience is in any way an unknown quantity, despite efforts to find out about them from the organizer, then choosing the degree of formality may be a problem. Some audiences like being addressed in an informal and conversational manner, while others expect the speaker to keep his distance, as it were, and not treat them to a cosy chat when they expect a well-prepared address. The decision will often depend on how many people are present. It would be insensitive to deliver a speech from a lectern with all the formality and remoteness of a large public meeting if you were speaking to a dozen ladies in a village hall, for this situation would obviously demand a much more personal and conversational style of speech. It would be equally insensitive – and ineffective – to give your views on juvenile crime in a casual conversational style if you were addressing five hundred people in the town hall.

The most sensible approach is to imagine you are on the platform in the hall where you have been booked to speak and are addressing the audience which the organizer has described to you. Then write out your speech as though you were at that moment speaking it under the exact circumstances you have pictured in your mind. In this way, your speech will be appropriate for that particular occasion and the style of language – formal or informal – will automatically suggest itself.

It must be stressed, however, that it is essential to choose words that are genuinely 'you' and that will enable you to communicate fully with your audience. These two things are not necessarily the same and you may have to modify the first in order to achieve the second. This is well illustrated in a story concerning George Herbert the seventeenth-century poet and preacher. He came from a distinguished career at Cambridge to be the rector of the little country parish of Bemerton, near Salisbury. On his first Sunday there, he treated his parishioners to a full-blown university sermon, like those that had made his reputation at Cambridge. This was *his* style and language and he was being true to his own manner of preaching. But he looked at the faces of his congregation and knew beyond doubt that, although he was being true to himself, he was not communicating at all with his rustic flock. He concluded his sermon with a promise that he would never address them in that way again, and he kept his word.

George Herbert learnt the lesson that the language that came naturally to him was an impenetrable barrier between his parishioners and his message. It is a lesson to be heeded by all public speakers, especially those who lecture on specialist subjects such as science, technology, economics, psychology and even the arts. All these subjects affect the lives of people today and they want to know more about them. But the lecturer has to adapt his language to his audience and realize that he cannot take for granted an understanding of his technical terms or even his modes of thinking and expression.

Some inexperienced speakers (and, unfortunately, some who are experienced enough to know better) think there is a special public speaker's language, and they take refuge in it as a substitute for developing their own style. As they understand it, the style consists in using time-honoured phrases which flow from their pens and spring to their lips and, even though the origin of such phrases is lost in the mists of antiquity, they seem relevant and meaningful in this day and age. In other words, they resort to clichés – and the previous sentence contains six of them! Clichés are phrases that once were new and striking but have been used so often as to become tired and uninteresting. They are deployed by speakers who wish to give their words an air of importance yet lack the inventiveness to devise new phrases of their own. Undeniably many clichés are useful because they say exactly what we mean and save us the trouble of thinking of a different way of expressing it. There is no harm in the occasional use of such clichés, particularly ones that are really expressive and generally understood. 'He has a bee in his bonnet' is a vivid metaphor and widely known, but the language of a speech loses its freshness if pompous and hackneyed phrases occur constantly. The careless use of clichés can also give rise to unintended humour, as when an orator urges us to put our shoulders to the wheel and explore every avenue while we pull for the shore!

Politicians are notorious for using overworked phrases and for attempting to make simple statements seem important by using long phrases when a word or two would do. The much-used 'industrial action' sounds serious, dignified and menacing all at the same time, but the stark word 'strike' is honest and direct – and powerful. A political speaker may sometimes be wise, from his point of view, to wrap up his meaning in wordy phrases, because the plainly stated facts might repel. Too often, however, the wordy phrases are simply a smokescreen, and the frequent use of such phrases is the trademark of the windbag. Audiences are shrewd enough to see through such tactics. The best political speeches are those which appeal directly to the hearts and minds of the audience, using language that can be easily understood, and gives the impression – whether one agrees with the speaker or not – of an honest attempt to deal with the problem being discussed.

Nothing is more wearisome than the speaker who mouths the modish jargon of his profession or special interest. While bandying about the latest phraseology may be all part of the game of impressing your colleagues at a staff meeting or business conference, it will cut you off entirely from an audience to whom you are trying to explain the workings of your firm, school or association. Another obstacle, increasingly common these days, is the use of initial letters to indicate organizations, people and policies. We all know what is meant by the letters BBC, TUC and MP. But someone lecturing on modern education will quickly lose a lay audience if he starts talking, without explanation, of TVEI, NAB, CEO, PAT, NCPTA, MEP, UCET, PGCE and UGC. There are dictionaries of abbreviations, which are very useful – but an audience should not need to use them to make sense of a speech. If you find such abbreviations convenient, begin by using the complete phrase and then introduce the audience to the abbreviation, and revert from time to time to the full version to make sure everyone still knows what you are talking about. Even with an audience of professional colleagues it would be wrong to assume that everyone is up to date with the latest set of initials – though no one will want to reveal that he is behind the times by asking you for an explanation!

In writing your speech, watch out for words which are frequently misunderstood or confused. One very common error, for example, is to confuse 'flaunt' with 'flout'. 'To flaunt' means 'to show off', whereas 'to flout' means 'to treat with contempt'. Thus a speaker who complained of people 'flaunting the law' when he means 'flouting it' would be saying almost the opposite of what he intended. Close in meaning but still distinct are 'viable' and 'feasible'. The first means 'capable of life and development' and the second 'practical, possible'. Science has made a channel tunnel feasible and investors would see it as a viable business enterprise. 'Credible' and 'creditable' are easily confused – the first meaning 'believable' and the second 'worthy of praise'. To this pair may be added 'credulous', which means 'too ready to believe something'. 'Effect' and 'affect' are also frequently confused, but their similarity in pronunciation will often disguise the error.

Another trap to be avoided is the imprecise use of words. For example, 'unique' means 'the only one of its kind' and is therefore complete in itself and should not be qualified by other words, in phrases such as 'very unique' or 'extremely unique'. Something either is unique or it is not. Eric Partridge's *Usage and Abusage*, and of course a good dictionary, will help you to avoid traps of this kind.

Those who care for the health of the language they speak should guard against the sloppy use of words. Particularly in speech, words may be used for their emotive power in such a way as to blur their true meaning. A good example of this is the use of the word 'obscene'. It means, according to the *Shorter Oxford Dictionary*, 'offensive to modesty or decency', yet it has such powerful connotations that it is frequently applied to anything from a rival party's political programme to a lack of provision of pop music. A glance at any newspaper will provide similar examples. ('Democracy' can now mean almost any political system the speaker wishes.)

The English language is immensely rich and flexible, and capable of conveying every shade of meaning; those who speak in public should take pride in exploiting its resources and using it appropriately.

How to begin

The great importance of having a good opening to the speech has already been mentioned. Before we go any further, let's consider this in some detail.

Have you ever thought that the audience may be nervous too? They will not enter the hall with sweating palms and trembling knees (which may be your unhappy fate); but just before you begin to speak there is a subconscious anxiety on the part of the audience. Is the speaker going to be a success? Will he embarrass us by his inadequacy? Will we have to endure an hour of increasing boredom? Your opening sentences will either confirm these fears or put the audience at their ease, ready to settle back to enjoy themselves. It depends on your voice, your manner and your matter.

The first words you speak are vitally important in setting the tone of the whole talk. Ironically, these words are unlikely to have anything to do with the subject of your talk at all! Almost certainly they will be an acknowledgement of the chairman's flattering remarks with which he introduced you. You can of course acknowledge these with a curt, 'Thank you, Mr Chairman,' and then proceed with your speech. But this would be ungracious, to say the least, and would not make a good impression on the chairman or on the audience. You do not need to extend the courtesies unduly, but some remarks thanking the chairman for his generous references to you and expressing pleasure at being invited to address the audience would be in order. Do not improvise these remarks on the night, as this could give your talk a very uncertain start. It is better to have prepared an opening, though you have to make some small modification to it in the light of what the chairman says – or does not say.

Knowing what you are going to say from the start will give your voice the necessary strength and firmness. A mumbled hesitant reply to the chairman's greeting will depress the audience just when you wanted to make them sit up and take notice. Many speakers make the mistake of thinking that their speech begins when the preliminaries are over. The truth is that you are making an impression on your audience, for better or for worse, from the moment you rise to your feet, and the first words you utter signal all sorts of things to the audience about your manner, your personality and the quality of your voice. A clearly spoken opening, easily heard, confidently phrased and agreeably delivered will set at rest all the subconscious fears of the audience. It cannot be stressed too much that these opening civilities must be well prepared and should be regarded as part of your performance. Once you are on your feet, you have already started!

Having replied to the chairman, you make a very short pause to indicate that your speech proper is now about to begin. Then you deliver the opening remarks, to which you have given a great deal of thought. The object of the opening is to seize the audience's attention and concentrate their minds on you and your subject. It is a wonderful feeling for you, as speaker, to know that your first sentence has 'hooked' the audience, that their small shufflings have stopped and that every eye is focused expectantly on you. You have won the first round.

How you achieve this is partly a matter of personality and partly to do with voice, but it also has much to do with the right kind of opening for this particular talk. You have to consider your audience, the nature of the subject and your own personality. A shock opening would misfire badly if your voice and personality lacked the necessary drama; a comic introduction would fall flat if you lacked confidence in your own sense of humour. What is more, neither of these openings would be suitable if your talk was a severely practical address to a group of business associates. Make the beginning appropriate to yourself and to the context of your talk. You have several methods to choose from.

There is the simple and direct opening such as, 'I am going to talk to you tonight about home decorating.' This is unimaginative and unlikely to enthuse the audience, but it does state the subject of the talk very clearly, which is certainly a merit. It may also suit the practical nature of the talk which is to follow and signal to the audience that the speaker is a down-to-earth person from whom good practical advice can be expected. But even an audience intent on picking up hints for do-it-yourself jobs could be won over by more attractive openings.

A humorous approach is a special favourite for after-dinner speakers but it would not be out of place with a topic as strictly practical as house decorating. A brief and witty account of the disasters that have attended the amateur paper-hanger would amuse the audience and lead neatly into the subject. But humour needs to be handled with care. Not every funny story is guaranteed to go down well with every audience: what suits a business convention might not suit a literary study group. The humorous opening should be closely related to the topic that is to follow – and it should not be too long! It should also be immediate in its impact. Brilliant witticisms often need a second or two to work out, and you cannot afford this time-lag at the beginning of your talk. It will be very dispiriting if, when you have delivered your punch line, there is only a dubious titter of mirth from those who think they have worked out the joke, followed gradually by scattered laughter as more people latch on to it. What you want is a quick gale of laughter that tells you the audience is with you and you have scored your first hit.

Shock tactics are often effective: 'Every single day, healthy children living in your city are absorbing a slow poison that will kill them within fifteen years!' What can this be? The audience will be on the edge of their seats to know what dire kind of pollution is threatening their families. Statistics are often used in this kind of opening, stating how many thousands of people are dying from disease or starvation *at this very moment*. By presenting facts in startling relation to our own experience, a new slant is given to the subject and the impact makes a striking opening to your talk.

Everybody loves a story and you can be sure of your audience's interest if you begin with an anecdote. Often the climax will be humorous, but it need not be so. It may be moving, dramatic or simply thought-provoking, but it will have done its work if it gathers the audience to you and leads directly into the main part of your talk. Most anecdotes concern people and that is why they are particularly successful in gaining attention – we are eternally curious about other human beings. Every good journalist knows this, which is why newspapers are full of human-interest stories. Study the way articles in popular magazines begin and you will see how often they are introduced by a story in miniature. The advantage of such an opening is that it catches the attention because of its human interest and the universal desire to know what happened, while at the same time leading to the main theme, for which it already supplies an illustration. If the anecdote concerns the speaker himself, so much the better: the audience has the added interest of seeing before them one of the characters in the story and hearing about his part in the incident from his own lips. One warning – do not spin out the tale to unreasonable length. An anecdote is meant to be short and pithy and make its effect very rapidly. A classic example (said to be the shortest ghost story in the world) goes like this:

> Two men were sitting in a railway carriage.
> 'Do you believe in ghosts?' said one.
> 'Of course not,' replied the other.
> 'Well, I do,' said the first man – and promptly disappeared.

Brief, amusing and very much to the point, this could be the introduction to a light-hearted talk on ghost-hunting – or on strange companions!

Another well-tried device is the challenge, often phrased as a rhetorical question: 'Have you ever considered that you create more pollution in a year than your grandparents did in a lifetime?' 'Can you sleep comfortably in your beds tonight knowing that today a thousand animals have died in research labs for your sake?' 'Do you believe that TV violence is corrupting your children. You do? Then why haven't you sold your TV set?'

This kind of approach is intended to stir the audience and set it thinking. From its very nature, it is abrasive. The audience is not made comfortable by questions like these, but for some speeches you do not want your audience to be comfortable. Your job is to shake them out of complacency, make them change their attitudes and move them to action. You want to make them feel as indignant as you do over injustice in the world, cruelty, pollution, or whatever. You are not there to cocoon them from reality and allow them to pass a pleasant hour. Your motive is quite different from that of the speaker who has come merely to entertain. Therefore a challenging opening will be very appropriate to your purpose.

Once you have used this opening, you have the task of bringing the audience to your side. The opening was intended to arouse people's feelings of guilt and shame, and these are not comfortable emotions. You should not go on bombarding your listeners with such challenges so that they grow increasingly resentful as the speaker seems intent on giving them a brisk dressing-down. The knack is to turn the challenge in such a way that the audience feel there is much truth in what the speaker is saying and that they would like to join him in putting matters right.

A situation of this kind will arise in a political speech and here the challenge can often be derived from the policy your opponents are putting forward:

> 'The leader of the — party told us last week that when he comes to power the standard of living of every family in the land will rise by 10 per cent. But he won't tell us who is going to pay for this. But I'll tell you, my friends. It is *you*, the working people of this country, if you allow yourselves to be fooled by promises which can't be kept.'

This opening is direct, hard-hitting and straight away takes the war into the enemy's camp.

Speakers nowadays are less inclined to indulge in scholarly and literary allusions than they used to be, but a striking quotation is still a good way to start a speech. In a political speech, it might be a remark from one's leader, designed to enthuse the party faithful, or a scornfully delivered quotation from the opposition, followed by a scathing comment, to arouse mirth or murmurs of agreement. On less highly charged occasions, the quotation from literature might still find a place; a browse through a book of quotations will yield a number of treasures.

To these suggestions of how to begin a speech may be added one or two remarks on how *not* to begin. Do not begin by apologizing for your own inadequacy. If it is true, the audience will find it out for themselves all too quickly. Probably it is not true, but is a nervous attempt to gain the sympathy of the audience. It will not work and it does not deserve to. Confidence breeds confidence. The audience wants to feel happy in the knowedge that you know what you are doing. If you begin by telling them that you are not too sure of your ability to address them, they will feel dispirited and uncomfortable, and your chance of winning them to you with an effective opening has been completely thrown away by this nervous disclaimer.

Another opening to avoid is the one which directs attention to all the paraphernalia you have brought with you and which is *not yet ready*. When the chairman's introduction is over, you should rise to your feet, place your notes on the desk at once and begin to address the audience. If, during the welcoming applause, you open a brief-case, drag out a pile of unsorted papers, shuffle through them, look for your spectacles, find them, wipe them with a handkerchief and then blow your nose, the audience will be less interested in what you are to say than in what you are going to do next!

Your opening remarks set the tone for the whole speech. Make them effective and you have given yourself a flying start. Do it badly and you will have to struggle to recover the confidence of your audience and – which may be more difficult – your own confidence.

And how to end

A good ending is obviously of the greatest importance in the success of a talk. It is not that your last remark will necessarily be what lingers longest in the minds of your listeners. To be honest, the important points in the middle of your speech may be better remembered – and rightly so. It is just that a good conclusion gives a satisfying sense that the structure has been completed, the shape of the talk made plain, with the beginning and the middle now rounded into a whole by the well-made ending. Really it is an artistic satisfaction for both speaker and audience, but it brings the very practical result that the speech is likely to be remembered with pleasure and not with the unease that a weak ending would induce.

The great thing is to ensure that your speech neither peters out nor comes to a sudden stop. The speaker who goes confidently through his speech and then without warning sits down because he has nothing more to say startles the audience and leaves them unsatisfied, as does the speaker who seems to be filling the time with points of less and less interest and finally fades away with no attempt to pull the speech together.

Some speakers think that an offer to answer any questions is sufficient to signal the end of the talk. While this can be successfully integrated into a conclusion, it may be better to leave it to the chairman to throw the meeting open to discussion. Then the speaker can concentrate on producing an ending which makes a thoroughly satisfying conclusion to his talk.

The kind of ending you choose will depend very much on the nature of your talk. If you are urging a case and arguing strongly for a certain course to be followed, then you will want to end with a rallying call for action. The intention will be to make the audience enthusiastic to do something in your support. If your talk has been an appeal for charity, then you will make a last urgent plea for a sympathetic response from your audience. If, on the other hand, your talk has been largely informative and descriptive, you need to leave the audience feeling that they have enjoyed exploring the areas you set out to present, and that you have shaped the talk clearly. This can often be done by a general remark about the topic as a whole, perhaps followed by the modestly expressed hope that you have done a little to reveal the interest that lies in this particular subject.

To be effective, the conclusion should not be too long. That is why no speaker should feel compelled to summarize all he has said in the last three minutes. The conclusion is not a summary; its purpose is to leave the audience with a satisfying sense of completeness. Only in a situation where it might be useful to recall the two or three main arguments in favour of a course of action should a summary be considered. This can then be capped with a call to action.

Now you have gathered the material, made your initial jottings and pruned them to suit the approach you have decided on; you have also considered the shape of your talk and the appropriate style of the language. Now there is nothing for it but to take up your pen and begin to write the speech itself.

Good luck!

9 When you have written the talk

It may have taken you three hours or it may have taken three days, but the speech is finished! There it is on paper at last and you know that whatever lies ahead, you have something you can present to the audience when the great day comes. The relief is enormous because up to now you may have had the nagging thought that when you came to compose the speech you would not find enough to say. Now you know that you probably had too much to say and the speech is already far too long. What are you going to do about it?

Initially, nothing. Put the speech away for two or three days and try to forget about it. This will allow your mind to clear and other matters to fill your thoughts. Very probably ideas about the talk will pop into your mind during this period and if they seem worthwhile you can jot them down to consider later. But on the whole it is best to give the mind a break from the concentrated work you have just done. When you return to the speech it should be with a fresh eye and more objective perceptions.

This is the time for personal criticism and revision. When you read the speech through after the break of a few days, you are almost sure to come across words and phrases that seem wrong, sentences that sound awkward, perhaps a whole section that strikes you as missing the point. This is only to be expected and no cause for disappointment. Every speech-maker, like every writer, expects to revise and correct the first draft of his work, improving this part and jettisoning that. As you read through, you may mark in the margin places you will need to return to for a detailed rethinking, but do not stop to do this now. It is important to gain an impression of the speech as a whole. So read straight through and listen with an inward ear to the sound of the speech, because you are dealing in oral and not written communication.

If you are so inclined, you can read the speech aloud to yourself straight away, but it might be better to go through it once silently so that you can take in the shape of the whole argument more quickly.

Once the immediate revisions are over, there will be opportunity to try it aloud.

What is vital at this early stage is to be sure about the timing. There is no need to read aloud the whole speech in order to time it. You can gain a good idea of how long your speech will take by reading aloud just one page, timing this and then multiplying the result by the number of pages you have written. When you do this, it is important to adopt the pace and style of delivery you will use in public: reading through to yourself as you sit at your desk is likely to be quicker than when you stand up and talk to an audience. The result of this timing exercise may well startle you. It is a common experience to find you have written too much. Something will have to be cut out.

This often proves a hard decision. We all become rather attached to what we have written, especially if we have taken trouble over it. We also tend to think that every line of our script is quite essential for the talk and we will be depriving the audience of something they really ought to know if we cut anything out. All very true, no doubt, but the demands of the clock are inexorable; you have been asked to speak for forty minutes – and forty minutes it has to be. If you sit down after thirty-eight minutes, you will have succeeded brilliantly. If you drag on for fifty, then the audience – and chairman – will be looking at their watches. The best compliment is for someone to say, 'I was amazed to find your talk lasted for forty minutes. To me it seemed only half the time. I could have gone on listening to you all the evening!'

To achieve this accolade you must prune. Have a look at your introduction. You know that this is a most important section and perhaps for this very reason you have given more space to it than you should. See if it can be shortened without losing the effect. The chances are that by tightening it up you will improve its impact.

Look too at the conclusion. Have you tried to pack in too much because you knew the speech was coming to an end? Have you tried to summarize everything you have already said? If so, this is almost certainly unnecessary and an opportunity for cutting.

When you are satisfied that the beginning and the end are as you want them, see if there are too many examples or illustrations in the text. They are of course a necessary part of your speech, which might be dull without them, but two or three may have to be sacrificed in order to get the timing right.

If all this pruning still leaves the speech too long, then you will have to review the main sections. Obviously you are trying to include too much and so you will have to be ruthless with yourself. If the talk was intended to be informative, you will have to number the main points of information in order of importance and then delete the least interesting. If you were arguing a case, look for the weakest point in your argument or what seems likely to be the least impressive and get rid of it. (The result will probably be a sharpening of your attack.)

In all these ways you can reduce the length of your talk and bring it within the limits you have been allowed. If you are still rueful about having to discard some of your material, remember that there will be a question-and-answer session after the talk. Some of the points you had to delete may well arise at this time. It is far better to leave an audience wanting more than to spoil an otherwise good talk by simply going on too long!

10 Rehearsing

Do you memorize your speech or don't you? This is where the experts differ. Some take it for granted that once you have written and polished your speech you then proceed to commit it to memory. Others shake their heads at this; they believe you should only learn the outline and then improvise the words that will give flesh to the bare bones. It is worth thinking quite hard about this. Do not decide too hastily that the safest way for you is to write your speech and then memorize it. Far from being the safest way it may be the high road to disaster. An audience likes to feel that the speaker is talking directly to them, using lively speech rhythms, conveying his own personality with spontaneity and vitality. They want to feel that there is no barrier to communication and that the speaker is personally committed to them for the duration of the talk. Freshness, liveliness and sincerity are what they look for, and anything which stands in the way of this has to be avoided.

The chief obstacle is the written script!

That is why it cannot be too often repeated: *you must not read your speech.* However good it is and however good a reader you are, that sheaf of papers comes between you and the audience and automatically inhibits that freshness and directness you want to display. Added to this, the written script will affect your stance and the use of your eyes. There is an art in reading aloud to an audience and it can be done very effectively (see Chapter 27, 'Reading the minutes – and more'), but a reader sets out to communicate a *written* text, usually composed by somebody other than himself. You, as a public speaker, are giving your own thoughts and experiences – and in your own words. Therefore your personal speech is an essential part of the presentation. It must be heard to be a living thing, apparently being created at the moment you are speaking.

This is a tall order for a beginner. But it is something that he has to accept. There can be no escape for him in reading aloud what he has written. Of course everyone knows that there has been writing during the preparation of the talk, but the audience wants to forget this and simply enjoy the speaker talking directly to them. Reading is therefore forbidden.

Is speaking a completely memorized script very much better? The answer is no; it is far too close to reading aloud. The speaker will be in the situation of reading a script which is printed in his mind instead of on the paper in front of him. The result at worst could be a stilted delivery, a glazed expression, a brow furrowed with the effort of recall or an unnatural fluency which says to the audience, 'He's repeating it parrot-fashion, like a child at school.'

The real disaster would come when, despite all the rigorous efforts at learning, the memory lets the speaker down and he suddenly 'dries' in the middle of his speech and is left groping for words that simply will not come.

There are arguments on the other side, of course. A beginner may feel more at ease if he knows his speech by heart; it does not have to sound stilted, and an irretrievable breakdown is not very likely. Yet there is an element of surrender in this attitude. It is surely better to begin your speaking career as you mean to go on – by firmly accepting the principle that *you do not memorize your speech*.

How then can you be sure of what you are going to say?

The answer is to become thoroughly conversant with your own written text, reading it silently a number of times with the aim of memorizing the steps in the argument *without trying to commit to memory the precise words in which they are couched*. Of course the written words are your own words and – if you have followed the advice given earlier – they have been written as spoken English of the sort you yourself would expect to use. Therefore a great many of the phrases and sentences will be in your mind and readily available when you make your speech. But you will not be repeating them mechanically. They will occur spontaneously at the moment you need them and if you give the speech on another occasion they may arise in a somewhat different form. The result will be that the audience will have no feeling that you are simply repeating a memorized text. You will be seen to be talking to them untrammelled by a script, whether written on paper or photographed in your mind.

As your object in this study is to master your material without learning it off by heart, you should not read the text too many times, otherwise you *will* begin to memorize it. What you are trying to learn are the main points in the structure, together with the back-up material that supports each. Be sure of the sequence in your own mind and the words will come.

It must follow from this that rehearsing your speech out loud over and over again is not recommended. This can set up patterns of words and speech that will lead to the kind of delivery you are anxious to avoid. Of course you will need to try out the speech in the privacy of your room and if you encounter serious problems during that attempt you will have to deal with them and then rehearse again. But limit yourself to two or three run-throughs. In this way you will keep the freshness and spontaneity that are the hallmarks of a good speech.

11 Notes

Here is a challenging thought: *do you really need notes at all?*

Many experienced speakers would feel quite lost without their notes and would violently oppose any suggestion that they are unnecessary. Yet if the sequence of points has been well learnt and one thing leads naturally to the next, then it could be argued that notes are far from essential and are in fact something of a barrier, albeit a small one, between speaker and audience. If visual aids – maps, diagrams, exhibits and suchlike – are used, then these alone will provide the reminders that the speaker may feel he needs. (See Chapter 14, 'Using visual aids'.)

On the other hand, notes are a great confidence booster and no beginner should be without them. They give confidence not only to the speaker but also to the audience. One can imagine the uneasy feelings of an audience who sense that the speaker is a beginner and then realize that he has neither notes nor script at hand if anything should go wrong. It may be that the speaker will find he does not need to refer to his notes, but at least they are there and this gives him reassurance. There is a story that the great tenor, Count John MacCormack, had a favourite encore. He had sung it hundreds of times but he always held the words on a card in his hand. One night he went on stage without the card – and broke down. The psychological support given by the existence of notes should not be lightly discarded – though the night you decide to leave them in the greenroom could be a landmark in your career as a speaker.

Assuming you are going to use notes – and you would be foolhardy to abandon them at the start of your career – what form should they take?

There are two main kinds: those written on one or more sheets of paper and those written on cards. There are many disadvantages in using sheets of paper. They tend to be floppy and untidy to hold; unless secured, they can litter the table or even blow away – and they can tremble visibly in a nervous hand. Because of the size of the usual piece of paper, you may be tempted to write too many points on it and then have the problem of locating the next item when you want it. The card method is distinctly preferable.

For this you need half a dozen cards of about postcard size or a little larger. On the first card write the title of your speech and on the back note down any equipment or visual aids that you need. This card is essentially a label for the whole set when you file it away. Take the other cards and number them clearly in the top right-hand corner. Card number one should contain the form of address with which you will open your remarks. If this is simply, 'Mr Chairman, ladies and gentlemen' you may feel it is not worth bothering about. But if you have a distinguished company with a list of titles, it is essential: 'My Lord Mayor, Your Grace, Your Excellencies, My Lords, Ladies and Gentlemen . . .' A stumble at this moment or the omission of a title is not worth risking.

If you are following other speakers who are talking controversially on the same subject you should keep the second card blank. This is so that you can note down any points from previous speeches to which you want to reply. Such points are best dealt with without delay so that they do not interfere with the run of your well-prepared speech. You will have to be the judge of where it is best to make these replies. Probably you will want to start with the opening you have already devised, but immediately after this you may be able to insert your remarks to counter or support what has been said by previous speakers. The notes for this are available for you on your card – but it will cause an embarrassing hiatus if you cannot read your own handwriting!

This brings us to a most important point: your notes must be absolutely clear and easy to read. Some speakers rely on a typewriter, using capitals for the main headings. Others feel that this is too small and prefer to write in block capitals with a thin felt-tip pen. You will have to be able to read your cards without continually whipping your glasses on and off – which would annoy the audience and distract them from what you are saying – so if you normally use reading glasses, you may have to write large enough for you to be able to read what you have written *without* your glasses. (If you intend to do a lot of public speaking, you might consider getting bifocals.)

It is essential to have ample spacing and to avoid putting too much on one card. Guard, too, against making the notes into a mini-script. They are an aid to memory and nothing more. Their job is to remind you of the next point in your argument and, at most, to give you two or three supporting details. This should be more than sufficient to keep you on the rails and enable you to move through your speech with confidence.

It will be a matter of personal judgement how many points you can put on one card. It may be only one or two, and is unlikely to be more than four. A typical card with two main points on it would look like this. The subject of the talk is 'Why We Need a Supermarket', and this card would be in use about half-way through the speech

LARGE PARKING AREA
— ease of access
— convenient for loading shopping
— the bonus of free parking
ENVIRONMENTAL IMPROVEMENT
— site at present derelict
— architect's designs exciting
— promised landscaping of surrounding areas

Before you come to use your cards, you should decide where you are going to place them during your speech. One solution is to hold them in your hand, glancing down at them as necessary, and quietly placing a used card at the bottom of the pack or on the table. Shuffling the top card to the bottom should be done with care: an ill-judged movement could scatter all the cards and cause chaos. Placing the used card quietly on the table is better, but if the action is done fairly often (which it need not be), it can become distracting and the audience will feel as if they are watching the sand fall through an egg-timer. The higher the pile on the table grows, the nearer they are to the end of the talk!

To have notes lying flat on the table carries serious disadvantages. It means that every time the speaker wishes to consult them, he has to bend down to see what is written, so losing eye contact with his audience. The best arrangement is to have a sloped reading-desk or lectern at a height convenient for the eye of the speaker, yet not so high as to become a barrier. The ideal situation is for the speaker to be able to glance quickly at his notes without dropping his head.

When a card has fulfilled its usefulness it can be gently pushed from the main pile to one side and the relative size of the two piles is not seen by the listeners. However, many halls will not be equipped with a lectern and the speaker will have to make do with what is there. If he arrives in good time, as he should, he may be able to devise something suitable for himself, using a small pile of books, for example. He might even have the foresight to bring two or three volumes of an encyclopaedia with him in his car to create a make-shift reading-desk. Some have found that a good-quality music-stand, with a thin board or piece of card as backing, makes an excellent reading-desk, especially as it is completely and easily adjustable. It is also very portable.

The physical attributes of the speaker also have to be considered. A very tall person will be tempted to stoop down over his notes, while a very short person may look lost behind a massive lectern; if he wears bifocals, this, too, will make a difference to the placing of the speaker's notes. This is further evidence of the need to arrive at the hall in good time, so that adjustments to the lectern can be made or a substitute found.

On many occasions there will be no lectern and the speaker will have to hold the cards in his hand. After all, the hands are the most instantly adjustable of all reading-desks. But the speaker must take care not to fiddle with the cards or draw attention to them by waving them about or flexing them nervously in his hands.

Think of your notes as discreet friends, waiting quietly to come to your assistance when needed, but not drawing attention to themselves in front of the company.

3 Giving a Talk

12 The day arrives

Most talks are delivered in the evening after the speaker himself has already done a day's work. If you are booked to make a speech, try to pass your working day so that you are reasonably fresh for the task ahead. What you most want to avoid is a hasty scramble after work to grab a meal, change your clothes, put your notes together and travel to the hall where you are going to speak. You can help yourself in this matter by planning those last hours well ahead. For example, you could finalize your preparation of your notes and visual aids the night before and leave them all ready for you to take with you when the time comes. Decisions about the clothes you are to wear and your travel arrangements can all be made well in advance, so leaving you with less to worry about at the last moment.

Try to give yourself ten or fifteen minutes' rest before you leave for the meeting. Use the time to perform one or two relaxation exercises, some deep breathing and a few warming-up exercises for the voice. Then quietly look through your notes, just to give yourself confidence that all is under control. If you have to undertake a long journey by car, then you can warm up the voice as you drive alone – but do not overdo it. You want to arrive at the hall fresh, not vocally tired out!

Although you will certainly *not* be reading your speech, it is probably good for your confidence if you put it into your briefcase along with your notes. You know very well that you are not going to use it, but there just might be a moment of anxiety before the talk when you want to check on a detail that does not appear in your notes. You will also be taking any visual aids. What else you take along will be up to you. Some speakers would not be without a favourite brand of throat pastilles; others like to take along a hairbrush and comb. One elderly lecturer, eccentric, but very famous, used to startle the organizer by opening his bag and producing a small bottle of brandy with the remark, 'And this is to revive me if I should collapse'!   You must allow yourself plenty of time to arrive at the hall so that you can be there well before the start of the proceedings. There are things to be checked, especially if you have never been to the place before, and you must avoid a hasty entrance with no time to catch your breath before you are rushed on to the platform to make your speech.

Presumably the organizer will be there to greet you — you will have discussed with him the time most convenient to you both for your arrival. After exchanging civilities, move on to the preparations you wish to make. If your host is inclined to chat when you want to be checking the stage or asking necessary questions, you must use tact to steer him towards the matters you wish to deal with. These will include the arrangements on the platform. You will be lucky if you find a lectern all ready for you. The chances are that you will have a flat table and an upright chair. If you wish to improvise a reading-desk, using books to support your notes at a height which suits you, this is the time to do it. Perhaps you have materials to display or visual aids to set up. All this will need time and discussion with the organizer — hence the importance of arriving at the hall in good time. You should try to get all these preparations done before the audience begin to arrive. It is unsatisfactory if the principal speaker is seen fussing around on the platform, moving furniture and so on, while the audience come in to take their seats.

You may be fortunate in having the luxury of a 'greenroom' in which to spend the time between your preparations in the hall and the moment you go on to the platform. This is where you could do the relaxation and deep-breathing exercises already mentioned, and where you can finally make sure your notes are in order and your appearance as you would wish.

Technical equipment presents special problems — it can so easily go wrong! If you are using a slide projector, for instance, you must try it out in the hall before the talk begins and have it all set up and ready well in advance. A microphone needs to be tried out and a decision made as to whether or not it will be helpful to use it. If you require a cassette- or record-player to provide aural illustrations for your talk, it is essential to test it in the hall, as the acoustic may be quite different from what you expected. Small details such as the absence of a cable long enough to reach a wall socket can ruin well-laid plans for the use of equipment. All these things need fore-thought, time enough to sort them out and contingency plans if the equipment cannot be used or fails to operate. It is better to have at least some idea about how you will proceed if your machines fail you than to leave it completely to chance and try to extemporize. Few of us have the skill of the comedian Tommy Trinder who, on a night which will never be forgotten by those present – at a troops show in Burma during the Second World War – found the hall plunged into darkness by a power failure and had the audience rocking with laughter as he ad-libbed for nearly an hour in the dim light of a single hurricane lamp!

If you are an after-dinner speaker or the guest at a luncheon club, then circumstances are different from those of the speaker in a hall. There will be no question of arranging a lectern and so forth. You will probably be speaking from the place where you have had your meal and will be seen as a member of the company – albeit a special one – rather than as someone elevated on a platform. All the same, the advice about early arrival still applies and, as far as circum-stances permit, you will do what you can to assess the room in which you are to speak and the place you are to speak from. Before the meal you will no doubt be introduced to several people and will have to make conversation with them, as you will with your neighbours during the meal. While this is not necessarily the ideal preliminary to speech-making, it has its advantages. You make the acquaintance of some of the audience in advance and gain useful impressions about the attitudes and interests of those to whom you are going to speak. It is most likely that the friendliness of your hosts will help you to relax and make you feel that the event is going to be less of an ordeal than you supposed. Obviously you will take care over what you eat and – more especially – over what you drink. While the company should be happily relaxed with their wine and cigars, you have to be clear-headed!

You rise to your feet . . .

The chairman makes his introductory remarks, the applause gives you an encouraging welcome and you rise to your feet. This is the moment all the thought and preparation have been leading towards. You have to put into practice all you have read and all you have rehearsed, and the vital moment is – now!

It is vital because the way you deliver your opening is going to set the tone for the whole presentation. The audience are waiting to assess the kind of evening they are in for and they will make all sorts of judgements on the strength of your first two or three sentences. You must therefore get them right.

The first rule is not to rush. Wait for the applause to die down and any rustling to subside before you begin to speak. A few seconds of silence will gather the audience to you in a mood of expectancy. Keep your head raised to them as you wait to begin and do not fuss with your notes. You should give the appearance of relaxed confidence as you stand there with a pleasant smile on your face (unless your subject is too serious for smiles!), exuding an air of quiet assurance. Your first words (which will probably be an acknowledgement of the chairman's introduction) should be spoken quite slowly and firmly, but with a bright tone and in a gracious manner.

The controlled pace not only makes for good communication with the audience: it counteracts your own nerves which may be trying to hurry you on. It also helps to establish your authority. This is what the audience is looking for and when they sense it they will at once accept that you know what you are doing and they will be prepared to listen to you with interest.

Choosing the right steady pace is not enough. It is just one element in the fundamental requirement of *audibility*. However many good qualities a speech may have, they are reduced to nothing if the speaker is hard to hear. As one Member of Parliament has remarked, 'It's bad enough having to listen to MPs. It's even worse when you can't hear them.' The logic of that sentence may not be faultless, but the meaning is clear enough and it applies to all public speakers. You owe it to your audience to be audible. If you gain a reputation for being difficult to hear, you should not be surprised if invitations to speak in public dry up very rapidly. It is from your opening remarks that your listeners will learn whether or not you can be heard easily. A hesitant, mumbled reply to the chairman will disappoint your audience and rob you of the confidence they were waiting to place in you. Therefore, a good breath, a steady pace and a well-projected voice as you begin your speech!

Audience awareness

As the speech proceeds, you must be continuously aware of your audience. This seems such an obvious remark to make that you may wonder if any speaker can forget the group of people he is addressing. But, surprisingly, it is possible to ignore the audience. At one extreme, you can imagine the cartoon figure of the bumbling professor, with his head buried in his notes, droning on regardless of the drooping eyelids and nodding heads before him; at the other end of the spectrum is the brash extrovert, so convinced everyone loves the sound of his voice as much as he does that he roars along 'full of sound and fury, signifying nothing'. These are caricatures of speakers insensitive in different ways to their audiences. But any speaker who grits his teeth (not good for clear speech, by the way) and drives on with his rehearsed talk, taking no notice of the way it is being received, will be a failure. Actors tell us that every audience is different and that part of their skill lies in assessing each set of playgoers and varying their performance subtly to take account of the people 'out front'. Stand-up comedians are past masters in this art, working on each audience in a slightly different way depending on their readiness to respond, their mood and their reactions. A matinée audience takes more warming up than an evening audience; a Monday show will be harder work than one on a Saturday night.

You will find the same thing as a public speaker. The quip that goes well with one audience will fall flat with another; the intricate point that needed careful explanation and repetition with one audience is instantly taken up by a different and livelier group. Therefore, when you speak, your antennae must be out all the time, judging the impact you are making. The signs are easy to recognize.

The most encouraging are the faces that are turned towards you, bright with interest and usually accompanied by the suggestion of a smile. Ready laughter, murmurs of assent and, in certain circumstances, bursts of applause give you the assurance that things are going well and the audience is very much with you.

If, on the other hand, the faces turned towards you begin to have a certain fixed look about them and one or two heads – and then several – begin looking towards the floor, you are having trouble. Looking away from a speaker, especially downwards, is often a sign of embarrassment: the listener is trying to pretend he is not present at a talk which, through its inappropriateness or obvious lack of success, is causing him to feel uncomfortable. Eyes that wander around the room or seek the greater interest of a programme or handbag signal boredom and the need for action on the part of the speaker.

Signs that things are not going well do not mean that the talk is necessarily a bad one. After all, you have discussed the topic with the organizers, you have thought, research, planned and rehearsed the whole presentation. Unless there has been a serious misjudgement, the talk is probably very suitable for the audience. The source of the boredom is far more likely to be poor delivery – and that includes lack of variety.

As soon as you become aware that all is not well with audience reaction, make a rapid mental check of your own performance. Inevitably the first question must be, 'Can I be heard?' An audience who realize that they are trapped for an hour in a hall where they are going to be tantalized by knowing that something interesting is being said but they cannot hear it are going to switch off and look for a more entertaining way of passing the time – such as counting the cracks on the ceiling. Therefore make sure your voice is carrying to every part of the hall. Along with this, check the speed at which you are speaking. If you are going too fast, the audience will be wearied by this flow and bored because they are unable to absorb what you are telling them. They will be equally bored by too slow and ponderous a delivery, with long gaps between the remarks and a leaden pace. So audibility and speed are the first items to check and, if necessary, improve.

If you feel that these basic elements are not the cause of the trouble, then the most likely explanation lies in the monotony of your delivery. What you need is variety. One way to achieve this is to vary the pace of what you are saying. As you approach an important point, make yourself slow up: speak the key sentences with deliberation and marked emphasis. Then, when the point has gone home, speed up your delivery (not too much, of course) as you reinforce the point with explanation or illustration. This swifter pace itself will be drawn back a little later into a steadier movement – and so on throughout the speech, varying the pace from time to time so that there is no danger of a soporific drone.

Varying the pitch of the voice is equally important. It is unkind to your audience to speak for an hour or so, using a range of only two or three notes in the middle or, more usually, the lower part of your register. No one expects you to fling your voice up and down the scale like a Victorian ham actor, but those troupers did at least make use of their full vocal range – and often to pretty startling effect. If you feel that your voice has been pitched on too low a note for rather too long, make a point of deliberately pitching the voice higher as you begin the next speech paragraph. With the natural tendency of the voice to fall, it is always a good idea to start the next section at a slightly higher pitch than the one you have just finished with. You could devise a special sign to put on your note cards to remind you of this from time to time.

Variety of intonation is also very necessary. Unless your natural speech is impossibly monotonous and inexpressive, you already use considerable variety in the intonation (or speech tunes) that you employ in normal conversation. The intricate patterns of the rise and fall of the voice convey meanings and feelings of great complexity in everyday speech. When you speak in public, allow these natural intonations greater freedom of movement than would be necessary in ordinary talk. Just imagine how you would say to another member of your family, 'Are you going to put up with this?' and then think how the vocal range for this same speech tune would be widened if a skilled orator said this at a public meeting. You will have to judge for yourself the degree of expansion needed for your particular audience. An open-air rally will need far more vocal range for its speech tunes than a small meeting in a private room.

With these resources at your disposal to banish monotony, you will soon begin playing on your audience – deliberately drawing back the pace as your approach a really telling point, dropping the pitch to a more solemn note for something very serious and signifi- cant, and using a lively range of intonation as you tell a funny story or make a humorous aside. But you still have a most impressive device to deploy – the pause. Did you notice how the dash before the last two words of the previous sentence held you back in sus- pense for a split second even as you read it? This is the effect of a pause; when you speak rather than write, you become the master of the precise timing, judging exactly when to release the tension of the audience by proceeding.

A pause occurs naturally at the end of a speech paragraph or main section and should not be ignored or rushed over. The audience, as well as the speaker, are grateful for a moment of rest before renewing concentration for the next point. But the pause has other and more spe- cific uses. It can be employed after a particularly thought-provoking remark, silently inviting the audience to ponder the significance of what has been said. It can be used with considerable effect immediately *before* such a remark. This interruption of the natural flow of speech signals that something of special importance is to follow. An air of expectation and suspense is created and the audi- ence is put on the alert. Like all devices, this must be using sparingly, since constant repetition dulls the effect of such techniques; but if the pauses are judged rightly, they are invaluable.

There is something else you will discover soon after you rise to your feet. That is the acoustic of the hall. If you have the opportunity, try it out before the meeting, speaking a few sentences in full voice. Some halls are marvellously friendly to speakers, making it easy for voices to carry without effort; others echo like a bathroom or reflect no resonance at all. You can never be sure of the acoustics, however, until the audience are in their seats. The solid mass of their bodies is an acoustic factor and will often helpfully dampen an over- resonant hall or, conversely, deaden a building that seemed nicely responsive before they arrived. You can judge a great deal about a hall from the speeches or introductory remarks that precede your speech, but only when you begin talking can you be fully aware of whether the acoustics are on your side or not. If the hall is echoing or over-resonant, then you will have to modify your pace and volume to take account of this. If it seems that you are talking into a blanket, then you must use more vocal energy to get across to the audience. Just to complicate matters, a speaker cannot always tell how his voice is sounding in a particular hall; it is not unknown for a hall to seem difficult to a speaker when in fact he can be heard clearly by the audience. Not a great deal can be done about this, short of planting one's wife or husband in the audience to give a thumbs up or down sign. If the hall is large and cavernous, it is helpful to select a spot on a side wall some way down the room and direct the voice there, so that it is reflected back from a hard surface. The acoustics of heavily curtained rooms may be improved by drawing back the drapes – again evidence in favour of early arrival at the place where you are to speak.

Hands and eyes

Once you are on your feet and the talk has begun, two very basic questions will cause you some uncertainty unless you have thought about them in advance. What do I do with my hands and where do I look?

A simple piece of advice about the hands is to keep them still! If you are holding your notes, then keep them steady and do not fiddle with them, flex them or wave them about. If you are holding the sides of a reading-desk, then keep your hands there until you have definite occasion to move them. Beyond this, you will have to decide for yourself. You can put your hands behind your back, but this looks rather stiff and military, and a man who grasps the lapels of his jacket will look rather pompous and Dickensian. Either allow the hands and arms to hang naturally by your sides or place the hands lightly on the table in front of you, moving them to adjust your notes as necessary and to gesture if this is what you have decided to do at certain moments in the speech. The best advice of all, however, is to forget your hands and let them do whatever seems most natural.

The answer to the question, 'where do I look?' should be easy. You do *not* spend the evening with your eyes down on your notes or gazing at the sides of the stage. You look at your audience. But this does not entirely answer the question. Audiences may be large, they may be spread across a very wide room or scattered thinly in too large a hall. In any case, do you look over their heads or try to look into their eyes? During a long speech you will naturally look at several places in the hall; but the important thing is to maintain eye-contact with your listeners. You do not have to address every remark straight into the eyes of one or other member of the audience, although you will on occasion. At other times, you will let your eyes travel slowly across the ranks of your listeners as you speak. What is important is that the audience should be able to see your eyes for most of your speech. Choose a spot on the back wall just above the heads of the audience and use this as a kind of anchor point for your eyes to which they can return after looking elsewhere. As always, the appearance of relaxed naturalness is what you want to achieve. Eyes eternally fixed on one spot at the back of the hall will be as unnerving as eyes which for the whole talk restlessly dart hither and thither across the audience.

Body-language

There is no greater mistake than thinking that communication is entirely a matter of speech. In recent years there has been considerable research into the way we transmit our feelings and attitudes to others without saying a word. The position of the shoulders, the tilt of the head, the firmness of the knees, the angle of the torso tell us volumes about a person before he opens his mouth. A mime artist makes vivid use of this body-language to act out complete comedies and tragedies without a single word being spoken. The way a person walks into a room, sits in an armchair or reaches for a newspaper conveys a silent meaning, and we are constantly interpreting these movements and attitudes as we react to what we see. In the old days a soldier could be charged with 'dumb insolence'. The excuse, 'But I never said a word, sarge,' cut no ice. The offender's body-language had convicted him.

You, as a public speaker, must be fully aware of what your body and your movements are signalling to the audience both before and during your speech. What you wear is especially important. If you are attending a civic dinner or a society wedding you have no problem. For some functions the dress may be specified on the invitation. But if you are giving a talk to a public meeting, a learned society or a social club you will have to give some thought to the way you will dress. Standards are less exacting than they were: for men an open-necked shirt no longer looks casual or sloppy, though it would not be appropriate for every speaker or every audience. A lady in trousers would have been unthinkable a few years ago; now she might seem to be highly fashionable – at any rate to some audiences. It really does depend on the audience. It will not do for a speaker to say to himself, 'This is how I dress: they must take it or leave it.' He is forgetting that the moment he walks on to the platform his appearance is telling the audience something about him and the audience will interpret what they see in the light of their own attitudes and – yes – prejudices. Therefore if you are seeking to win over your listeners, there is no sense in antagonizing them at the start by dressing in a manner that will not please them.

This is not to say that you must always dress with the greatest formality. Far from it. A student audience will accept that an elderly professor should speak to them in a dark lounge suit, collar and tie (and academic gown?) but a young lecturer will feel more at ease – and so will his listeners – if his dress is indistinguishable from theirs. If, in contrast, he should take pains over his appearance, dressing elegantly and expensively, he will be saying something about his own character and his feelings of the difference between himself and his students.

Your choice of dress should also be appropriate to your subject. If your talk includes a demonstration, then this may decide what you are going to wear. A track-suit would be right for a talk on physical activities and sport, illustrated by exercises which you will yourself perform. A cookery expert might don an apron for some or all of the presentation and a science lecturer might need to wear a lab coat. But whatever you are wearing, do the audience the courtesy of making the best of your appearance. If you are careless of how you look, you are telling the audience that you do not think much of them.

Make use of the way you walk on to the platform and the way you sit during the introductory remarks to give the audience confidence in you. A brisk businesslike entrance and an alert posture as you follow what is being said makes you already an active participant in the proceedings rather than a passive spectator.

Your body should not distract the audience's attention away from what you are saying. Good posture will give you a feeling of well being and provide the correct basis for the management of your vocal resources; and it will also present an agreeable appearance to the audience. If you allow yourself to droop over the table, round-shouldered and bent-kneed, you are conveying weakness and a lack of confidence in your own power to communicate.

Above all, keep still! Unnecessary movements and monotonously repeated gestures irritate an audience, and the speaker who wanders aimlessly about the platform quickly becomes a bore. Of course there is a place for movement and gesture in your speech, but it must be intentional and purposeful, not the result of your own nervous agitation. It is impossible to lay down strict rules for the use of gesture because it must always appear natural and therefore should arise from the deeply personal body-language of the speaker himself. Some extroverts use a good many hand movements with their everyday conversation, as if words alone were not sufficiently expressive; their hands are brought into service too to reinforce what they are saying — 'If you tied his hands, he would be dumb.' If fluent gesture is natural to you there is no reason why you should not use it in your public speaking; it would probably be difficult to stop you. But if you know you are prone to a frequent use of gesture, you should question how far it is really necessary and with the aid of a friend (or a video) find out to what extent your gestures are a help or a distraction.

The most convincing movements will arise when you are handling your visual aids or demonstrating with equipment. This is because you are acting quite naturally and, incidentally, are more relaxed than you would be standing at the rostrum. It is fascinating to see how much more at ease a less experienced speaker becomes when he moves to handle the equipment.

While easy, natural body movements and gestures are acceptable and even desirable during a speech, the wandering lecturer definitely is not! Some speakers simply cannot stay in one place but stroll up and down the platform, lingering only briefly here and there before resuming their endless perambulations. The biggest distraction from the speech is the speaker himself. The audience is constantly on edge, not knowing where he is going next. Not only does this restless movement spoil the concentration of the listeners: it may affect the speaker's audibility when a microphone is being used. Unless he is holding it in his hand, the situation becomes impossible. Furthermore there is a mesmeric quality about such movement as the heads turn this way and that . . .

A hint which may be of use to those who cannot stand still in one place for more than a few moments is this: press your thighs lightly against the table in front of you and maintain this contact while you are speaking. Once you feel the pressure going, gently re-apply it; otherwise you will be drifting from the table and wandering about in your usual fashion. No one need be aware of what you are doing and it should gradually become natural for you to stay where you are!

How many speakers remember that what goes on under the table may be fully visible to the audience? This is a curious thought, but not an unimportant one. A speaker who stands with crossed feet, swings on one heel or is simply weak-kneed looks feeble and unconfident – and an open table provides no cover for this. If the platform is fairly high, the audience will have a full view of the speaker's legs and feet under the table. Firmly planted feet will not be remarked on, but legs that cross and uncross or swing backwards and forwards will begin to fascinate the audience, who may find their changing patterns more amusing than what is being said! The rule is to stand up straight with your two feet firmly and naturally placed on the floor.

Facial expression also plays an important part in your presentation. Again, it must arise naturally from what you are saying and cannot be imposed artificially. But since you are interested (as you surely must be) in your own material, let this be seen in your face and manner as well as in your voice. A show of enthusiasm is infectious. A dismal face and drooping body is no advertisement for the interests you are trying to share with your listeners.

The central feature of your facial expression will be your eyes. As already explained, use them to establish and maintain eye-contact with the listeners, and avoid the temptation to hide them by looking down at your notes on the table.

There is no getting away from the fact that when you are a public speaker you are on show. The clothes you wear, your hairstyle, your posture and your movements all speak eloquently about you to the audience. Make sure they say what you want them to!

13 Question and answer

'Our speaker has kindly agreed to answer any questions you would care to put to him. Who would like to begin?' The chairman smiles hopefully at the audience – and there follows a long and embarrassing silence!

This is because the cosy feeling one has as an anonymous member of the audience is threatened when one is invited to stand up and ask a question. Just for that moment the questioner himself becomes a public speaker with all eyes turned on him, and there is an understandable reluctance to be the first to submit oneself to this ordeal. Once somebody else has broken the ice it takes less courage to ask a question. It is for this reason that an experienced chairman will have a question of his own ready and waiting. He may do the audience the courtesy of inviting their questions and then pausing briefly to see if anyone is ready to speak. If a member of the audience responds immediately, it is a good sign that other questions will soon follow and the chairman can reserve his own question until there is a lull. If, however, there is no response within a few seconds, he can save embarrassment to both the speaker and the audience by putting his own question first. With this encouragement other questions are likely to follow and the discussion section is successfully under way.

If you are a new speaker, you may feel a little nervous about this part of the proceedings. Perhaps you will be asked something you do not know; perhaps an expert in the audience will pick you up on something you have said; perhaps the fluency in your speech that came from sound preparation will desert you when you have to speak impromptu. These nervous fears are unlikely to prove true in the event. A flurry of questions is an excellent sign that the talk has aroused interest and thoroughly engaged the attention of the audience. There is also likely to be a more relaxed atmosphere during this part of the evening, with you, the speaker, able to respond to individual members of the audience. Your answers will be of added interest to the audience as a whole and you may well learn something about your subject which you did not know before.

To make this session the happy and productive part of the presentation that it should be, remember that it is intended for *all* the audience and not merely for the individual questioners. If there is any chance that a question may not have been heard clearly in every part of the hall (and this is very probable), then you should repeat the question before you answer it. In replying, address your remarks to the whole audience and not just to the questioner. It is no fun for the rest of the audience to sit straining to hear what you are saying while you happily chat one-to-one with a questioner in the front row.

Try to answer the question simply and informatively and guard against allowing yourself to launch out on a digression that gets further and further from the point. The time allowed for questions is almost certain to be limited and it is unfair to other members of the audience who are queuing up with their questions to allow that time to drift away while you ramble on in response to a single question. Your chairman should be of use here, controlling the questions and limiting the individual who, having asked one question, tries to ask several supplementaries or even make a speech himself.

If you realize that the chairman is leaving the session entirely to you, you will have to select the questions yourself. It is best to do this politely but firmly, indicating the questioner to whom you will reply by word or a gesture rather than standing passively while two or three questioners jockey nervously, unsure who is to speak.

If the talk has been controversial, there may be hostile questioning but, in view of the nature of your speech, you will be prepared for that. If you feel you have a strong case, you will stick to your guns and reply, using your authoritative knowledge of the subject to score another point. Avoid being dragged into detailed discussion of trivial or obscure points and, above all, keep your temper. In a political meeting, for example, some questioners and hecklers will be anxious to destroy your self-control and will set out to do so. If you allow them to succeed, you will seriously weaken your case and damage your standing in the eyes of the audience. With good humour and shrewd replies you should be able to turn the tables on your opponents and this will greatly enhance your position with the audience.

Sometimes you will come across the questioner who has simply missed the point of what you have said or who appears not to have been listening at all! Avoid the temptation to score off such a questioner. An appearance of arrogance will not go down well with the audience. Just give a simple reply, gently referring to what you have already said in your speech.

If you are asked a direct question and you do not know the answer, then say so. There is nothing to be said for bluffing it out. No one can be expected to know the answer to every possible question and audiences understand that. If you are able to suggest where the answer may be found, pass this information on to the questioner.

During the question-and-answer session some speakers choose to remain seated. Unless there is some special reason, such as age, infirmity or a very small room, it is best not to do this. Your answers are an important part of your presentation and they should be treated as seriously as the talk itself. It is more effective if you stand well when replying to questioners and your audibility and audience contact will be much better if you are on your feet rather than sitting back in a chair.

At the end of the session, when time has run out or when no more questions are forthcoming, the chairman or some other person will say a few words of thanks to the speaker. Applause will follow and there is sometimes an awkwardness as the speaker sits in his chair, smiling uncertainly or nodding his head in a gesture of acknowledgement. It is far better for the speaker to rise to his feet and bow once to the audience and to the chairman and then prepare to leave the platform.

14 Using visual aids

'And what is the use of a book,' thought Alice, 'without pictures . . .?'
The same might apply to many talks. If you are going to speak in
public, remember that you can often enhance your talk by giving the
audience something to look at as well as to listen to. But there is a
great deal more to using visual aids than simply holding up a picture.
First of all, you have to make up your mind if you really need visual
aids. You are not likely to require them if you are proposing a toast
at a wedding or offering good wishes to a colleague on retirement.
But if your talk is intended to inform as well as to entertain, then
you should seriously consider whether what you want to say will
be made clearer and more interesting by asking the audience to use
their eyes as well as their ears.

All kinds of talks will be enhanced by visual aids – descriptions
of journeys, holidays at home and abroad, historical and scientific
talks, reminiscences, explanations of processes and how to make
things – all these and many more cry out for skilled use of visual
material.

If you decide that visual aids are right for your talk, you must take
them seriously. They have to be good to look at, effective for your
purpose and well integrated at the planning stage. *They are not mere
decoration.* Above all, visual aids must be visible. There is nothing
worse than being shown something that you cannot see clearly.
Many an inexperienced speaker will produce picture postcards of
what they are talking about and hold them up to the audience regardless of the fact that they cannot be seen in any detail beyond the
front row. What is even worse is to make a feeble apology, such as,
'I'm sorry you can't really see these cards: they are all that I've got!'
If that is true, then the speaker should not be showing them to the
audience in the first place.

Visual aids can take several forms. Pictures are the most obvious
and often the most useful, but maps, plans and diagrams all come
under this heading. Nor are 'visuals' necessarily two-dimensional:
exhibits of all kinds are included. These may be models, craft items

(partially made or completed) and all sorts of objects of interest relevant to your talk. If you are talking to a Women's Institute about cookery, for instance, you may have a chart on the wall behind you summarizing a process, an attractive poster showing the completed dish and, on your demonstration bench, the ingredients weighed out and ready, as well as examples of your dish prepared for the oven and also completely baked.

Nor does this complete the list of visual aids. Some speakers will want to show coloured slides to illustrate their talks; others will bring in live animals – and what about using another person as a visual aid? We will talk about the special problems – and opportunities – of these ideas a little later on.

Once you have decided that visual aids will play a useful part in your talk, it might be worth considering whether or not they can make your notes unnecessary. This will not always be the case, but if your visual aids are sufficiently comprehensive, you might find that you do not need notes in your hand at all. The exhibits will be sufficient reminder of what you wish to say.

Let's imagine that your talk is to do with visits to some wine châteaux in France. A map with the places clearly marked and joined by a line to show your itinerary will remind you of the sequence of your journey. On the table before you will be bottles, clearly labelled, from each of the wine areas. They will contain wines of different kinds and will probably differ in shape. Beside them you may have dolls in the appropriate costume of each area; you may also have other items relating to each region. The point is that these items, carefully arranged in sequence before the talk begins, will remind you of what you wish to say and the order in which to say it. Your visual aids have not only interested your audience and enhanced your talk, they have also become your notes!

It is worth spending time considering how you can best display your 'visuals'. Do you want them to be in view of your audience right through the talk? Quite possibly you do, but you might consider whether the unexpected production of an item or a picture might have a dramatic impact on the audience. In such an event, you would have to devise a way of keeping this item out of sight of the audience until you need to show it and of producing it slickly and easily, with no awkward delay while you struggle to get it from a suitcase under the table.

The obvious way to display a picture or chart is to pin it up. But before you casually assume that this is the easy part, you should make sure that the hall in which you will be speaking actually has a wall behind you – and, if there is one, whether the owners mind you sticking pins into it! You might have to request that some sort of display board is made available for you and it would be essential to arrive at the hall in good time to make the necessary preparations.

If you are using a series of pictures or diagrams to illustrate a developing process, then a good way to display them is to hang them from a set of rings so that they can be turned over rather like a loose-leaf calendar. For this, you need to be quite sure of the steadiness of the stand on which your pictures are to be displayed – this is something else to check before your talk.

To prepare a set of effective visual aids is only half the battle. You also have to use them efficiently. One of the commonest faults when using a drawing is to turn in towards it and give the talk with your back to the audience and your nose in the picture. This has a great deal to do with nerves. The drawing represents a way of escape from the audience, a refuge from their daunting eyes. You tell yourself that the audience realizes your need to look at the drawing in order to explain it and this becomes a wonderful subconscious excuse for avoiding their gaze. It may make you feel a little less nervous, but it destroys the most important element in your presentation, your contact with the audience and your command of their attention.

It is not really difficult to indicate things on a drawing and still remain facing the audience. All you do is place yourself on one side of the drawing and roughly parallel with it. If the item is fixed to a wall, then you stand with your back to the wall and only a little in front of it. You are now in a position to raise your arm and point to the place on the drawing you wish to discuss, simply glancing there to direct your finger (or pointer) to the right position but, for the most part, continuing to face the audience. There is no need to be rigid and artificial about this; the audience is prepared for you to look briefly at your own visual aid – but they will lose patience with you if you speak to them for more than a few seconds while looking at the wall and not at them.

With three-dimensional exhibits this danger is unlikely to arise. If you are speaking about, let us say, an antique vase, you will either have it on the table in front of you or else you will be holding it. You will therefore have no problem about facing the audience. What you have to be careful about (apart from dropping it) is to use it and then put it down. Nothing is more irritating than a speaker who continues to clutch an exhibit when he has gone on to talk of something quite different, particularly if he fiddles nervously with the object, thereby distracting the audience even further.

Another way to lose your audience is to pass an exhibit around *while you are talking*. This has the effect of completely distracting the attention of those who are handling the object or waiting for it to be passed to them. It also introduces a continual ripple of disturbance as the item goes from hand to hand. Finally some poor soul is left holding it – or else feels impelled to walk up to the front and hand it back to you, thus causing more disturbance. So do not pass things around during your talk; wait until the end and invite members of the audience to look more closely at the exhibits if they so wish and if it is convenient for you and the organizers to let them do so.

Every actor knows that an animal or a child will invariably steal the show, and such fellow performers are often less than popular. It is highly unlikely that you will bring on a child as a visual aid (children in the audience are a different problem), but you may feel that your talk on grooming cats will be all the better for having a docile pussy on the table undergoing your ministrations as you talk. A docile pussy? Even the most sedentary of felines have a habit of becoming mavericks when they are used to illustrate a talk. It is not so much that animals are set on stealing the show; it is just that they have an inborn potential for wrecking it. They can do this in quite the most simple and innocent ways: a dog who yawns pointedly in the middle of your longest sentence; a cat which insists on hiding inside your pullover or a white mouse which nips off the platform – the potential horrors are too terrible to contemplate.

Seriously, you must think very carefully before you include a live animal in your presentation. Decide just why you think it will enhance your talk and if there is good reason to bring one into it, plan carefully at what point you will show it, what use you will make of it – and how you can get rid of it again. The answer here could certainly be to have an assistant who will look after the animal for you when it is not needed on stage. It is courting disaster to attempt to give a talk while holding down the animal or even quietly stroking it. Even if it is completely peaceful and well behaved, beware! You have a rival. Half the audience will be gazing fondly at your pet and thinking how much more interesting it is than you are, while the other half will be quietly hoping that it will get up and bite you.

One more warning – be considerate of the feelings of your audience. Some people will go rigid with fear if you produce a snake in the middle of your talk, while others will shudder at mice, spiders and even moths. Of course these people will avoid your lecture if the subject-matter is known in advance, but it is hardly fair to an audience to liven up your talk on India by unexpectedly producing a python from your briefcase.

Remember that another person can be a visual aid. Perhaps your talk is about fashion, past and present. A living person, wearing authentic period clothing, would be far more striking than a picture or a dummy. Instruction in life-saving really does require a 'guinea-pig' on whom techniques can be demonstrated, as do a whole range of subjects on health, fitness and sport. Sometimes it is enough to ask for a volunteer from the audience, but it is usually better to bring your own assistant who has rehearsed and who knows exactly what is required.

Make sure you introduce your helper to the audience graciously and remember to thank him or her briefly afterwards, allowing the audience to applaud if this is appropriate.

Finally a word about showing coloured slides by way of illustration to your talk. The large and beautiful pictures that can be projected from good slides make them a very useful resource for the speaker – but be sure that the slides really are good ones. Audiences are accustomed to seeing professional pictures of a high standard on their television screens, so do not inflict on them your under-exposed mistakes on the grounds that they are the only pictures you have. It would be better to concentrate on giving vivid descriptions than to disappoint your audience in this way.

Take account of the fact that some slide-projectors can be noisy. You do not want to spend a good deal of time straining your voice to be heard above the whirr of a machine. It is a good idea to plan a definite part of your talk when slides are to be shown. Before and after this, the hall lights will be switched on and you will give your talk in the usual way. Above all, do not show a slide every so often, switching the projector and the hall lights on and off at intervals throughout the session. Slides are a very useful adjunct, but like all visual aids their use must be carefully planned and controlled. If you are giving a whole evening of coloured slides, then you are giving a different kind of talk and this will be discussed in Chapter 16, 'Slide talks'.

All in all, visual aids are most valuable additions to the speaker's resources. But, as always, careful thought, planning and rehearsal are needed if they are to be really effective.

15 When it is all over

The chances are that, despite all your initial fears, your talk went reasonably well. The audience seemed interested, laughed in the right places and applauded you warmly at the end, and the chairman's words seemed genuinely enthusiastic. He may even have said he hoped to book you again one day.

As a result of this, you may be tempted to file your notes away without a further glance and look forward confidently to more invitations when word gets around about how good you are. You would be wrong to do so. It is important for your future as a speaker that you spend some thoughtful moments assessing your performance. This will be time extremely well spent.

Look through your notes, recalling how each section of the talk was received. You may remember that one part in performance seemed longer than you had expected and that you felt you had to hurry to get it all in. Elsewhere you may have been too brief and concentrated, so that you were left with the impression that the audience did not entirely follow your argument. There may have been a bad moment when a well-prepared joke fell flat or another when you lost your way and your notes were not clear enough to put you right. In every case, make a note to yourself to improve this when you next give the talk.

You should not concentrate only on your shortcomings. Write a little letter to yourself about the good points as well as the bad and file it with your lecture notes. When you are next invited to give the talk (which may be several months later) it will be encouraging for you to read that, generally speaking, the talk went well, that the audience responded particularly well to a certain anecdote or seemed very interested indeed in the exhibits that you used. The letter should also remind you of the improvements you felt to be desirable. Be completely honest and self-critical, so that however well the talk went at its first hearing, it will be that much better the second time you deliver it.

Self-assessment is essential, but unfortunately we cannot see our-

selves as others see us. A well-disposed friend or relation on whose
opinion you can rely will be an enormous help in the post-mortem
on your speech. He or she will be able to tell you objectively, but not
discouragingly, how you appeared to the audience. Perhaps your
eyes wandered disconcertingly or your voice dropped too low at
the end of sentences; you had a tendency to move away from the
microphone and this varied the speech level from time to time, or
perhaps your habit of scratching your nose became irritating. It is
things like this that you may have been quite oblivious of: 'Surely I
didn't do that?' you say in disbelief. But the honest friend was out
there in the audience and saw it happen. You will have to do something about it.

4 Special Subjects

16 *Slide talks*

The one kind of talk where the speaker should, quite literally, disappear into obscurity is the slide presentation. After all that has been said in this book about the importance of eye-contact and personal appearance we come at last to a situation where the speaker is, for the main part of his talk, simply a disembodied voice. The attention is turned away from him to a screen attractively filled with pictures, often brighter and more highly coloured than in real life, and the audience are informed and entertained principally through their eyes. Or so it might seem. Yet the pictures, however delightful and fascinating in themselves, are meaningless in the context of the lecture without the very skilled commentary that you, the speaker, will be providing. The slide talk is not a picture show. Nor is it a lecture with illustrations. It is a combined presentation of sight and sound in which the visual and aural elements are of equal importance. A single picture will save you paragraphs of explanation; a few words will give rich meaning to an otherwise uninteresting picture.

When you plan your talk, your question should be, 'How can I use both words and pictures most effectively to convey what I wish the audience to know?' The wrong approach is to say to yourself, 'I want to show some of my lovely colour-slides and I suppose I'd better say a bit about them.' A set of slides, in other words, does not release you from the obligation to plan your talk as thoroughly as ever. On the contrary, it demands skills of presentation of the highest quality.

A very common topic for a slide talk is travel at home and abroad, but there are many other subjects which lend themselves to this treatment – nature and the environment, popular science, the fine arts and practical processes of interest to do-it-yourselfers.

Once you have decided to use slides as well as the spoken word for your talk, the question arises: What slides shall I use? There is one quick and decisive answer to this: Use excellent ones! You must not inflict on your hapless audience slides of an inferior quality. There is sometimes a great temptation to use the only slide you possess on a certain aspect of your subject, even though photographically it is a poor one. Resist this temptation unless the point is very important indeed and you are quite unable to make it in any other way – which seems improbable. The pictures should be as clear and professional as the words and you should be rigorous in your selection of both.

Strive for variety in your selection of slides. A series of distant views will become boring: intersperse them with close-ups and middle-distance shots. Close-ups are particularly effective, as they are usually striking in themselves and enable you to comment with precision on details. It often requires great self-discipline on the part of a photographer not to show all the slides he has taken; but you have only to think of those evenings of suffocating boredom when a neighbour insisted on showing you his holiday slides – yes, all one hundred and fifty of them. So be ruthless in selecting only those slides that are relevant – and good!

This brings us to the question of the number of slides that should be shown during a lecture of, say, one hour. This depends on how long you allow one picture to stay on the screen. Naturally this will vary according to the use you wish to make of a particular slide, but roughly speaking one should allow any slide a *minimum* showing of fifteen seconds. If you move on more quickly than this, members of the audience will feel rushed and will be unhappy that you have snatched the picture away as they were still exploring it. One minute is the average length for showing a slide and commenting on it. Sometimes you will allow yourself a little more time and sometimes you will need less, but a slide outstays its welcome fairly quickly, particularly with modern audiences accustomed to the ever-changing pictures of television. You can say a great deal in one minute. If you want to say more, it is better to change the slide to another aspect of the same view and this will allow you to extend what you were saying without the audience losing interest with what is on the screen. The number of slides to be displayed in a showing lasting forty minutes should be between thirty and fifty.

Although you are going to spend a good deal of the evening as a voice in the darkness, you will begin with an introduction to your subject with the lights on and the audience able to see you. They are going to be in your hands for the next hour and this is their chance to get to know you before the lights are switched off and the projector is turned on. Your opening should therefore follow the same lines as for any other talk. Once you have made the initial contact, you can give the background information necessary to open up your subject and put the slides in context. As the audience have been promised a slide talk, the first section should not be too long – perhaps ten minutes at the most. From then on, the presentation will be the expected combination of picture and word.

While you should always identify a slide briefly, do not waste time by putting into words what the audience can see for themselves. Your job is to draw attention to the significance of what is being seen or to use it as an illustration of a point you wish to make. For instance, if you are showing a picture of a native woman coming from a pool with a water-pot on her head, it would be silly to say, 'This is a native woman coming from a pool with a water-pot on her head.' The audience knew that before you spoke. What would be worth drawing attention to would be the fact that men never did this task, that the pool was a good half mile from the village and that the women made the journey at least three times a day. In this way the significance of the picture is extended and you make important points about social attitudes and problems.

Some lecturers, when they want to indicate one particular part of a picture, will use a wooden pointer (not always easy to see) or a cunning device that allows a little illuminated arrow to dart around the screen. Although amusing and sometimes effective, this is not really necessary. You should be able to describe quite clearly where you want the audience to look and this has the advantage of giving them something active to do, such as finding the sculpture of a monkey at the bottom of the left side of the doorway to the church. These small tasks of identification counteract any possible somnolence that might be induced by semi-darkness, a warm hall and the lecturer's voice.

Changing to the next slide presents no difficulty if you are operating the projector yourself, using a remote control. But sometimes you are too far away to do this and have to rely on an assistant. He or she may have been instructed by you and know just when to move on to the next picture without any special prompting. But it is more likely that your assistant will never have met you before and will need to be given a cue for changing each slide. Rather than saying 'next slide please' over and over again, use cue phrases which become part of your talk, such as 'we now move on to . . .', 'the next slide shows . . .', 'let's now look at . . .' or 'I would now like you to see . . .' An alert assistant will have no difficulty in responding to this.

Your own position in relation to the screen requires some consideration. Try to avoid standing at a lectern near the screen with a reading-light illuminating the lower half of your face, making you a spectral distraction from the pictures you are displaying. As the whole presentation is one big visual aid – for you as well as the audience – there is no need for you to have illumination at all. You know your talk and each slide becomes a reminder of what you have to say, so why should you need notes? If, as described above, you direct the audience where to look by word of mouth, you can be well away from the screen in whatever seems to you the best position for audibility. The projector may be a noisy one and then you will have to be a good distance from it and close enough to the audience to overcome its whirr. A microphone may be available and this would remove any doubts about your being heard. The best kind to use is a hand-held or lapel mike because it will enable you to turn freely towards the screen or to the audience without loss of sound.

Early arrival at the hall is an absolute essential if you are giving a slide talk because there is so much to check. In addition to the usual pre-talk checks on the size of hall, the acoustics, your position when you speak, the lighting and so on, you must test the projector and, if you are to use one, the microphone. Be absolutely sure that both are as you want them and seek the opinion of the organizer or the committee about the best positioning of the screen, the projector and yourself. Check that your slides are correctly loaded and the slide-magazines are placed ready so that there is the minimum delay in changing to the next set. Check too that the cables for the power supply will not trip up members of the audience when they come into the hall, and that there is no danger of the plug being jerked from its socket or the projector from its stand. If you are using your own projector, make a point of taking a spare bulb with you. It might be needed!

17 The political speech

Politicians are the storm-troopers of public speaking. For them every speech is a small battle in the campaign for political power and when a politician speaks he is out to win. It is this that gives zest to his public life: a real politician thrills at the prospect of the hustings, the cut and thrust of debate and the challenge of a big public meeting. Some would say that times have changed and the days of town halls packed with excited crowds at election meetings are long past; it is easier for people to stay at home and watch the party leaders fight it out on television. This may be true up to a point, but no politician can stay at home himself. He has to be out and about, talking to people, knocking on doors and addressing public meetings. These may be less well attended than they used to be, but no one can make a career in politics unless he is able to stand up and speak effectively, and today a politician's platforms are likely to include radio and television studios as well as the back of a lorry.

Contrary to cynical belief, the first quality needed for a successful political speaker is sincerity. Audiences are quick to detect the man or woman who is simply repeating the party line with a patent lack of conviction. No party can be right all the time, and if there are details in a policy which the speaker himself cannot support, he will gain more respect and understanding for his honestly expressed reservations than for attempting to argue a case he does not believe in.

Sincerity is being true to yourself, and the aspiring political speaker should reflect this by using the language that is natural to him. Any attempt to make yourself sound like one particular leading party official or senior politician whom you admire will make your performance seemed forced and unnatural. Of course it will pay you to study the way experienced public figures make their speeches, but the only way forward for you is to develop your own personal style and not to ape someone else's.

No one these days likes listening to long speeches and so you should aim for the maximum impact in a short time. A speech that drags on and on will become less and less successful with every tick of the clock. Remember that there are probably other speakers waiting their turn. The audience wants to hear them as well as you, so make your points and then make way for the next person. Ten minutes or so will be quite long enough for a speech on a local platform: twenty minutes would be a really major effort. Discuss your contribution with the chairman beforehand and be guided over length by his experience and knowledge of the locality.

Have your points clearly planned and avoid repeating yourself. You will succeed best if you limit yourself to two or three main points and no more. Audiences can take in only so much at a time. You will be remembered if you are clear, direct and not repetitious.

The importance of a good opening has often been mentioned in this book. It certainly applies to the political speech. More than most speakers, the politician needs to get the audience on his side – that is why he is talking to them. The first remark must seize their attention. It may be humorous, dramatic or challenging, according to the subject in hand, but it should be designed to bring the audience to the speaker at once. For this purpose, a local allusion is often helpful, particularly if you, the speaker, have come from elsewhere. There is always some suspicion of outsiders coming to tell the locals what to do. A friendly reference to the town where you are speaking, especially if it shows some real knowledge of the place, will do much to encourage a welcoming response.

One problem you may encounter is that the audience have really only a hazy idea of the complexities that lie behind the issues you want to discuss. Very little in public decision-making is simple and straightforward, yet people like to think that there are instant solutions that politicians could bring about with the wave of a wand. As a political speaker you may have to counter these feelings by explaining the facts that lie behind a certain policy choice. You are in fact educating your listeners *but you must never allow them to be aware of this.* People have an intense dislike of being 'talked down to' and treated as though they were ignorant of matters that affect their lives. When you have to provide a background for your remarks, preface what you say with tactful expressions such as 'as you know', 'let me remind you', 'you will remember' and such like. This tiny lapse into insincerity may be excused since it is a courtesy to your audience, enabling them to learn some important facts without being made to feel that they were woefully ignorant beforehand.

As in all forms of public speaking, remember to address yourself to the whole audience and not to just one section of it. Something – perhaps a remark from the floor – may attract your attention to one part of the hall and you find yourself continuing to speak in this direction. You should correct this as soon as possible. Everybody in the hall wants to hear you and every single person wishes to feel he is worthy of your attention. If you continue to speak to one part of the hall only, you will quickly antagonize the rest of the audience.

A new speaker may not relish the prospect of questions from the floor and, worse still, heckling, but the experienced politician welcomes both these aspects of political meetings. If questions come thick and fast it means you have a lively and interested audience and you can reinforce your message during the replies. You are unlikely to be floored by a question because you will have done your homework well before you came to the meeting. With experience you will discover that you can anticipate the sort of questions you will receive and even the type of person who will ask a certain kind of question.

If you do not know the answer to a question, there is only one thing to do: you must say so. Any attempt to hedge or obscure the fact of your ignorance is self-defeating because the audience know that you have been caught out and they will despise your efforts to wriggle away. A straightforward 'I'm sorry, but I don't know the answer to that,' gains a few marks for honesty, but the bonus points will be collected if you quickly add, 'But I will find out and send you the answer if you will kindly leave your name and address.'

Heckling is the lifeblood of a political meeting and, far from being scared by it, the veteran politician genuinely welcomes it because it gives him more chances to score than it does to the heckler. After all, the speaker usually manages to have the last word. If every political speech is a battle, then heckling is the duel, the combat between two individuals, and audiences love it. Of course the speaker needs to have his wits about him and be able to think quickly on his feet but, considering his knowledge and involvement, he should have a ready answer for everything that comes. It is essential that he keeps his temper whatever is shouted at him and his best weapon is laughter.

If he can set the audience roaring with mirth at his opponent, then he has won the contest.

To succeed in politics you have to learn your trade as a speaker. There is no substitute for experience, which allows you to put into practice the good advice you have received from training courses or from reading this book. There are several public-speaking competitions run by the youth wings of the political parties and by business and educational organizations. By making use of these proving grounds you will learn your skills by practical experience. Then will come the opportunities to speak on real political platforms, and when an election comes along you can, to keep the military metaphor, win your spurs.

18 Talking to teenagers

Nowadays schools are very keen to encourage contacts with the outside world. To achieve this, teachers invite speakers from many walks of life to talk to their pupils on a great variety of subjects; those involving possible careers are especially popular. If you belong to one of the professions or are a member of the business or industrial community you may well be asked to speak to a school audience about your job. Representatives of sports and leisure activities find themselves welcome visitors at clubs and societies where they can inspire young people with their own enthusiasm. Organizers of charity appeals come into schools to explain their work, and on occasion representatives of political parties may be asked to expound their views to senior pupils or take part in debates on specific issues. An audience of teenagers is by no means an unusual one for a busy public speaker.

Although a school is the most likely venue for such a talk, organizations outside school – such as Scouts and Guides, youth clubs and church youth fellowships – also invite speakers. The atmosphere will differ from that of a school, but many of the same principles will apply.

There are two contrasting attitudes you should be prepared for, and you will recognize which one you are in for within a very few minutes of entering the room. One is exhilarating and one is depressing. The latter occurs when a class feels it has been pressganged into providing an audience for a topic in which it is not the least interested. Cynical boredom is the mood, and a sullen indifference to what you are trying to present. Let us say at once that you will be very unfortunate if this is your reception. You will have every cause to blame the teacher who has invited you for not preparing the ground better or at least warning you what to expect. But you are the one who is faced with the problem. Assuming that the pupils are sufficiently under control to allow you a hearing, you have to accept the challenge of arousing their interest despite their initial indifference. This is best done by keeping up your confidence in your own subject and taking the attitude that if you present your material clearly and interestingly you can bring the audience round. Unless you are a hopelessly dull speaker, you will find

that you will soon begin to engage their attention. Even in a very apa-
thetic audience there will be a few who are prepared to listen and if
they find you have something of interest to say the mood of attentive-
ness and responsiveness will spread. Humour is a great ally, but it
must be nicely gauged to the audience. Anything too subtle will be
lost and anything too weak will fall horribly flat.

Most audiences in schools will be far better than this. After all, you
start with certain advantages: a visiting speaker means a change from
classroom routine and the familiar personality of the teacher, while
the session is unlikely to be seen as 'work'. A visitor who has a successful career in the outside world commands a certain amount of interest
and respect – and there is always curiosity about a strange face in
the classroom. There may also be a general – if unjustified – feeling
that anything is better than another lesson from old so-and-so, their
teacher.

With these advantages on your side, you can approach the task with
some confidence. Your style will be less formal than with an audience
of adults but you must beware of trying to put yourself on the teenagers' level by using their slang or aping their manner of speech. With
teenagers this form of insincerity is fatal; if there is one thing they
resent bitterly, it is being treated like children. Teenagers are normal
human beings, very alert to what is going on around them, surprisingly well informed about certain things and generous in their
response to a speaker who interests them. However, they will have
less tolerance for any dull patches than an adult audience; their greatest condemnation is 'Boring!'

What really seizes the attention of young people is personal experience. There is so much that they do not know about the world and so
much that they are desperate to learn. Despite the avalanche of adult
experience poured over them by television, they welcome the chance
of hearing what life and work is like at first hand from a 'real' person
who has actually experienced it. If you are able to re-tell your own
experiences, whether in a job or a leisure pursuit, they will be keen to
listen, though any tendency to boast or show off must be resisted.

Take care to explain any technical terms you want to use and which
might be unfamiliar to the young audience, and be prepared to sketch
in any background necessary for an understanding of your subject.
Adults often forget that the personal experience of a teenager spans

a comparatively short time. Names and events of only ten years ago which are very familiar to adults may be totally unknown to fifteen-year-olds.

It should go without saying that clear speech is a first requirement. Schools are often noisy places: bells ring, feet clatter along corridors and doors slam. You should not have to shout to make yourself heard, but you should be prepared for extraneous noise and take pains to keep your voice audible.

The more you can do without notes the better. While it is acceptable for a lecturer to an adult audience to speak from behind a lectern and refer to his notes from time to time, with a youthful audience a more immediate contact is desirable. Teenagers respond readily to the speaker who will come around to the front of the desk and speak directly to them, with such command of his subject that notes are unnecessary. Of course if notes are essential to your confidence and accuracy, you must have them, but try to use them as little as you can. If you can bring some exhibits or other visual aids to show the audience, so much the better – providing they are well chosen and easy to see. An element of surprise is good too, such as producing an exhibit when it is least expected.

Question-and-answer sessions may take a little while to get started, as with an adult audience. For teenagers, the reluctance to ask a question may be a little more complex. They have a horror of making fools of themselves in front of their fellows; girls may not be very forth-coming with questions if boys are present. Of course it is impossible to generalize because so much depends on the school or youth club you have been asked to address and, frankly, a good deal depends on your personality and the response it evokes from young people. But if all goes well, the experience of talking to a teenage audience can be truly exhilarating, with an eager and intelligent audience warmly appreciative of someone who has come from the big world outside to talk to them. They will be ready with their laughter, serious in their questioning and warm in their applause.

19 Talking to foreign visitors

With the tourist industry booming and world travel becoming increasingly commonplace, it is by no means unlikely that a public speaker will find himself addressing groups of people whose native language is not English. Men in public life or running commercial concerns frequently meet visitors from overseas and entertain them at formal dinners or welcome them at official functions. Making a good impression on such guests is more than a social requirement: it could be essential for clinching a profitable deal with a firm or a locality.

The idea of setting up twinning links between towns in Great Britain and on the Continent, especially in France and Germany, has caught the imagination of many communities and it is very common to read two names on a road sign – one of the town you are entering and one of its Continental twin. This leads to valuable exchanges between the twinned communities with not infrequent visits of parties of citizens to each other's countries. Invariably there are receptions and entertainments, and local worthies find themselves making speeches of welcome or guiding their visitors around places of interest.

If a place is famous enough, there will also be conducted tours for parties of visitors from abroad, and the guide, professional or volunteer, will have to consider how best to cope with addressing an audience of foreigners.

Traditionally the Englishman abroad, if met with incomprehension, would try again, raising his voice and using stilted pronunciation, possibly with an attempt at pidgin English. The resulting lack of success only testified to the foreigner's imbecility!

Happily this kind of stupidity is seldom encountered today. If your overseas visitors do not know any English at all, then your speech of welcome must be very short and you must have an interpreter at hand. Long speeches in any language try the patience, but to inflict one on non-English speakers is plainly ridiculous.

In fact, the rise of English as a world language means that most foreign visitors have some knowledge of the language. Many of them will be very fluent and will put most Englishmen, who are inclined to be lazy about learning foreign languages, to shame.

Knowing this, you may be lured into the trap of believing that they can understand everything you say. This is most unlikely to be the case, since it is much easier to conduct a reasonable conversation about everyday matters in a foreign language than to follow a formal speech of some length and complexity or to take in all the information imparted by the guide taking a party round a historic house. It is a matter both of vocabulary and of grammatical structures.

Let us assume that you have to address a group of delegates from the Continent with their wives and husbands. The occasion is partly social and partly aimed at encouraging profitable business links between the two communities. You have to give the visitors a gracious welcome and you also have to tell them something about the industries in your area and the facilities, both commercial and recreational, that you can offer. The visitors know enough English not to need the services of an interpreter. How do you go about preparing and delivering this speech?

Bear in mind, right from the start, that clarity is the essential feature. This must be true of any good speech, but whereas an audience of English speakers can concentrate exclusively on the content of what you are saying, a foreign listener whose English is less than perfect must devote a good part of his attention to understanding the actual meaning of your words. Puzzling over words and phrases that he does not understand will cause him to lose the thread of what you are saying. Therefore, when you draft your speech, bear in mind the need for simple vocabulary and short sentences. If you are prone to use long words, then look for shorter and more familiar substitutes. Technical jargon should be avoided and any difficult expressions that are essential to your argument should be explained. Slang expressions may be entirely lost on your visitors.

When you have written your speech, even though you have borne these points in mind, go through it and see where you can make it even more simple and direct. Look out particularly for any complicated sentence with cumbersome subordinate clauses and when you detect one, re-write it, possibly using several shorter sentences to convey the same meaning. It is not necessary to reduce everything to the level of 'the cat sat on the mat', but you must put yourself in the position of a foreign listener and try and make it as easy as possible for him to follow what you are saying.

Above all, a foreign visitor will appreciate very clear diction. An English audience will probably be able to guess any words you mumble, swallow or distort, but you cannot expect the foreigner to do so. If he can instantly recognize the words you are saying, he will enjoy listening to you and will be gratified by his own command of English; but if he misses some words because of your imperfect diction, he will become frustrated.

Along with clear diction must go a steady pace. We complain that foreigners speak their own language too fast. Now the boot is on the other foot; visitors to this country will quickly lose the thread of a speech if the pace is too rapid for them. Adopt a well-judged public-speaking pace and then make it fractionally slower; you will earn the gratitude of your foreign guests.

Do not let your concern for clarity lead you into another kind of fault, a stilted and unnatural delivery. Those who learn a foreign language have listened to their teachers and to recordings of native speakers, and will expect to hear the intonation and speech rhythms that they are used to. If someone addresses them in too deliberate a manner, or introduces unnecessary gaps and pauses, the rhythms they are used to will be lost and their understanding will be impaired. When addressing foreigners, use simple vocabulary and short sentences by all means, but make sure you speak them clearly – and naturally.

The guide working in a historic house has an additional problem, as he has to say the same thing over and over again several times a day, and his delivery may become increasingly mechanical as the season goes on. With a party of native speakers, interested in hearing the bare facts, this may not be too serious; but with foreign tourists, rapid speech and an unvarying tone can be a handicap to their understanding and enjoyment. As already stated, clear diction (which guides usually have) and a steady but natural pace are what is required. Care should be taken not to assume a knowledge of British history or the dates of English kings and queens and their periods. Any reference, for example, to furnishings of the Regency period or to Tudor style may be meaningless to visitors from abroad. Similarly, technical architectural terms – postern, barbican, solar, keep and the like – should be explained. In a mixed group it would be advisable to encourage the foreign visitors to come to the front so that you can be sure they can hear you. This would have the added advantage that you could judge from their faces how well you were being understood.

Talking to foreign visitors is a great responsibility. It is an opportunity to promote international goodwill but, insensitively handled, it can lead to disappointment and even misunderstanding and resentment. Visitors to this country come here ready to enjoy what they find and eager to learn about our heritage and way of life. When someone addresses them, what they hope for is good plain English, spoken clearly and naturally – and not too fast!

20 The layman in the pulpit

The clergy are professional public speakers of a very special kind and it would be presumptuous in a book of this nature to offer them advice; students for the ministry are trained in this essential part of their vocation by experienced lecturers.

However, lay people are increasingly involved in reading lessons, leading prayers and also preaching, and these activities are not confined to those who offer themselves as lay preachers. It is no longer regarded as remarkable for a layman to be invited to address the congregation during a regular Sunday service. He may be the representative of a charitable organization or a lay worker in the mission field at home or abroad. Sometimes the vicar or minister in charge will invite laymen into the pulpit to speak about their own religious commitment. Apart from the Sunday services, there are other occasions during the week when laymen may be asked to speak to groups of church members on matters of their faith. This is public speaking with a difference.

Perhaps the principal difference is the relationship of the preacher to his audience. Whereas most other audiences listening to a serious speech have come specifically to hear the speaker and for no other purpose, a congregation has gathered primarily to worship God and hear his word. The sermon is one of several activities during the service, and not necessarily the principal one; any layman preaching at a service should realize that his sermon is just part of the whole act of worship. If a layman is invited into the pulpit, it will be because he has something special to offer from his own experience of life. He should therefore not hesitate to draw on this and refer to it in his address. His first-hand experiences, testing and strengthening his faith, will appeal more directly than any generalizations to the hearts and minds of the congregation.

Even if he has been asked to talk about the work of a charity or a similar church organization, the layman in the pulpit should never lose sight of the fact that he is preaching a sermon and, among all the interesting things he has to tell, his principal task must be to show how God's work is being done, recounting his personal involvement in it.

A layman may wonder if it is necessary to follow the tradition of beginning with a biblical text. This custom is no longer universal, but it does remind the preacher and his listeners that the ultimate authority for his words is the Bible and that what he says is, in its own small way, a further exploration of the Word on which their faith is based.

Much of the advice given in earlier chapters on preparing a talk holds true for the lay preacher as well. There must, as in all good talks, be a beginning, a middle and an end. But the sermon these days is much shorter than many other kinds of speeches: in reply to the young curate's question 'What shall I preach about?', his mentor said, 'Preach about God and preach about ten minutes.' Given the attitudes and attention span of modern congregations, anything more than twelve or fifteen minutes would be too long, especially for a lay preacher.

To convey a clear and effective message in this limited time takes skill and judgement. The first essential is to know exactly what point you wish to make and this will have to be sought in prayer and study. The theme could then be written down as a heading to your address and should be referred to frequently as you make your first notes and subsequently write out the sermon in full. With the key-note of your sermon thus constantly in mind there will be less chance of digression and obscurity.

Illustrations and anecdotes play an important part in a sermon. They can make arresting openings, immediately catching the interest of the congregation. To be really effective they should not be too long but should make their point before attention begins to flag. A long-winded tale with an ending which the congregation can foresee minutes before the preacher arrives at it is obviously counterproductive. Illustrations must be appropriate. There is no point in finding ingenious parallels between religious truths and common experience if the comparison is far-fetched and unconvincing.

There is no avoiding the fact that the personality of the preacher counts for a great deal in the pulpit. The layman who is invited to preach must offer himself to the congregation as he is, but with the humble confidence that he has been invited to preach because the vicar or minister feels he has something to say that the congregation will find rewarding. He should share his religious experience and insight with his listeners simply and sincerely, in words that come naturally to him, spoken clearly and unaffectedly.

21 Talking of science

Popular lectures, which did so much in the nineteenth and early twentieth centuries to inform the public at large of the exciting new developments in science, have largely disappeared with the rise of television as a medium of mass education. In the last century audiences flocked to the Royal Institution to hear Michael Faraday, whose brilliance as a lecturer paralleled his fame as a scientist. In humbler venues throughout the land, scientists with apparatus on the bench before them demonstrated the wonders of new discoveries and took their listeners step by step along the road to the new age.

In our own time the complexities of science and technology may be taken for granted, yet the sense of wonder has not disappeared – witness the huge audiences for popular science series on television, with amazing simulations of natural phenomena, superb photography and ever-changing graphic displays. These presentations are themselves triumphs of technology. There can surely be no place now for the lecture from the platform. . .

Yet such lectures do survive. The Royal Institution itself, where Faraday made his mark, continues a tradition, which has lasted for over seventy years, of children's lectures, and adult audiences still pack its famous Friday Evening Discourses. Up and down the land the *application* of science and its effect on our lives not only interest people but stir them to action when they feel their environment threatened. Great passions are aroused over such issues as nuclear energy and defence, pollution, the exploitation and depletion of natural resources, methods of animal husbandry and factory farming, and so on. There is a tremendous interest in natural foods and the effects of food technology on our eating habits and our health. Popular interest, in fact, has moved on from amazement at the sight of a taper burning in a gas-jar of oxygen to concern about the way the discoveries of science threaten as much as they enhance the quality of our lives. The modern scientist will therefore find himself invited to speak at meetings about the effects of new developments on the lives of ordinary people, and he can expect a keen and critical reception. The scientific lecture is still in demand but the emphasis has changed; people still want to know about the latest miracle, but they also want to probe the effect it is going to have on them.

If you are invited to speak to a lay audience about a scientific subject, you must make sure that the audience knows what you are talking about. What can be taken for granted in a university lecture theatre cannot be assumed in a village hall or at a chamber of commerce lunch. It may be that in order to make sense of an environmental problem you will have to educate your audience about the scientific processes that are causing concern. This will challenge you to find ways of communicating with non-specialists when you are bereft of the technical terms that make such statements plain sailing among fellow professionals. You will have to simplify and even over-simplify. As a good lecturer you will have to say the same thing in a number of different ways, with examples and illustrations, for the lay mind, unused to scientific thinking, will need time to absorb each step in your explanation. If one step is missed, then you have lost your listener for the rest of the argument.

To lead an audience into unknown territory you have to start from where they are. Find a point of contact between something they already know and what you want to explain. It may be some simple household application; it may be a piece of elementary scientific knowledge that is common currency. If you start in this way, it will give the listener confidence that he will not be taken out of his depths – even though it is your intention to take him quite a long way from the shore.

If your lecture is chiefly intended to educate and enlighten, rather than to support one side or other in a controversial issue, make up your mind what exactly you want your listeners to know by the end of the talk. They will not remember everything you have said; they will not be able to reproduce every step of your explanation, but they should go away with the feeling that what was a mystery to them is capable of explanation and that they have the ability to understand it. If they have to make a judgement on the way their own lives may be affected by it, they will have a background of knowledge on which to base their opinion. Therefore leave them, as far as possible, clear in their minds. Do not confuse them with side issues, extensions and ramifications. Concentrate on the basic principles involved and their application to the world beyond the laboratory.

Should you be called on to take part in a debate on a controversial issue – nuclear policy or experiments on embryos, for example – let your audience know that you too are a human being. The things that concern them are your concerns also, for you all live in the same world. Your scientific knowledge may give you a better understanding of the facts and of how the issues have arisen, and it will be your role to explain these; but nothing is more offputting than a superior attitude, the scientist-as-God approach. If you are to succeed in persuading an audience you must do it by a rational appraisal of the facts, the means by which all scientific progress has been made.

The more complex science grows and the further it moves beyond the comprehension of ordinary men and women, the more important becomes the role of the scientist as communicator. Inevitably, television is now the principal medium for the dissemination and discussion of scientific advances – and does it extremely well. But the lecturer addressing a small audience in a provincial hall still has a place. If he does nothing else, he both reminds himself and demonstrates to others that he is, and should be seen to be, a man speaking to men. He will find, however, that today people not only want to ask questions – they will answer back!

22 Judging competitions

You will not expect to find advice here on how to choose the finest pumpkin, the champion bull, the most talented dancer or the finest pianist – you will not be asked to adjudicate unless you are an expert in the field. However, the way you present your adjudication is also important, for you have the difficult task of rewarding the winners, without causing the others to feel discouraged.

After some competitions the judge is expected to do nothing more than announce the name of the prize-winner, but it is always much more interesting to the audience if he makes a short speech. This will have to be extempore because you, as judge, will not know what points you will be talking about until you have seen the entries. You will, however, as you go around the exhibits or listen to the competitors, have the opportunity to make notes about what you are assessing and you can ask for a few minutes on your own to make your final decision and decide the outline of what you are going to say.

When you stand up to make your speech and to give the results, you will probably be greeted with a round of applause. It has been truly said that the applause before the speech is to greet the adjudicator, while the applause at the end is for the winner. You then retire gracefully into the background, leaving the successful candidate to enjoy his moment of glory. Perhaps you, as judge, will also be asked to present the prize, and this will enable you to say a few words of congratulation privately to the winner before you leave the hall happy at a job well done or perhaps uneasy about the losers, whose eyes are shooting daggers at you as you leave the platform.

People do become very tense in some competitions, but a gracious and helpful speech by the adjudicator explaining the reasons for his final choice can leave even the losers feeling that justice has been done. The secret is to try and find something positive and encouraging to say about each entry. After all, each competitor has taken trouble to prepare for the contest. All have spent long hours on perfecting their entries: the very act of entering the competition has been an achievement in itself for some people. Therefore a judge who is dismissive in his attitude or uses his brief moment of power to show off his own superior knowledge while damning a competitor's efforts is letting down both the competitors and the organizers who did him the honour of inviting him to adjudicate. He is also discouraging people from pursuing their interest in his subject.

You will not of course give the result at the beginning of your talk. By holding it back until the end you keep the audience on tenterhooks as they follow each nuance of your remarks, trying to anticipate your announcement of the winner. However, since all that many of them want to know is the name of the winner, you must not try their patience too far by speaking at length. Five minutes should be the limit for this kind of speech, unless there are special circumstances to justify your taking more time over it.

Begin by expressing your pleasure at being invited to act as judge and see if you can find a compliment for the organizers on their success in arranging the competition. Then a general word of congratulation to all the contestants would be in order and an acknowledgement of what they have achieved. You should then move on to explaining what you have been looking for in the competition. This is interesting not only to those who have entered but also to the audience at large. Lay people are often mystified as to how a decision has been arrived at because they do not understand the finer points that are being judged. A huge vegetable at a country fair may appear very impressive to the uninitiated, but the judge will be looking at the small blemishes in the texture or discounting the entry because the vegetable is actually too big. A showy performance of a piece for violin may win loud applause, but the adjudicator will know that the player relies on a facile technique and has very little musicianship to back it up. So take the opportunity to explain the qualities you were hoping to find among the entries having regard to the conditions of the competition and, in the case of children, the age of the competitors.

It is important to bear in mind the position of those who have helped the contestants to prepare. In children's competitions parents and teachers are likely to be more emotionally involved than the children themselves for they will have invested much time and energy in fostering the children's interest in the subject. A wise judge will take care not to cause offence by his comments. He will need to tread carefully where teachers are concerned, since their livelihoods often depend on the success of their pupils in examinations and competitions; remarks which undermine the confidence of parents and pupils in their teachers should therefore be strictly avoided. Sometimes this presents a dilemma for the adjudicator when he knows very well that a child is being badly taught, but all he should do is comment as helpfully as possible on the deficiencies of the performance and how they might be remedied, without in any way undermining the teacher's position. This is not by any means easy, but it is not your job to come in as an outsider and injure the reputation of a local teacher.

If it is appropriate to comment publicly on each individual entry, be brief but positive. One of your tasks is to encourage participants to try again another time and to improve their standard. If a competitor leaves the hall saying he or she will never grow another turnip or play another piece because of your remarks, then you have failed abysmally. Everyone should go away determined to apply your advice and do better next year, full of enthusiasm for the art or craft you and the contestants are engaged in.

Time is too limited for you to do more than give a brief comment on each offering, so you should try to find one or two quite precise points where improvement can be made fairly easily. It is no good telling a gardener that his crop will improve if he moves to a different part of the country where the soil is better; nor is it your job to tell a drama student to change his technique from top to bottom. But a useful tip to the gardener on the best fertilizer for his area or advice to the actor on how to improve a certain kind of gesture will be welcomed and tried out. If you feel there is more you can usefully add, then you may be able to use an adjudication sheet on which you can write the additional advice that it would not be appropriate for you to voice in public.

When you come to declare the results, give them in ascending order with the winner being announced last. Make this your final remark and avoid any temptation to go on talking when the name of the winner has been revealed. The applause is for him and your task is over. But you may be invited back next year!

23 The toast is . . .

For many people, proposing a toast is the most likely way of becoming involved in public speaking. At the most modest level it may be nothing more than saying a few words and raising a glass to absent friends at one's own Christmas table. Family events such as weddings, christenings, birthdays and other anniversaries often include a moment when someone is called on to propose a toast. Outside the domestic circle, there are social and professional occasions when glasses are produced, the wine poured out and wishes for health and happiness conveyed in this time-honoured manner.

The custom of associating the drinking of wine with wishing someone well is long established, and is always conducted with some ceremony; in Shakespeare's *Hamlet*, King Claudius 'takes his rouse' to the accompaniment of trumpet, kettle-drum and cannon-fire. The connection between this kind of thing in royal circles and your breakfast toast and marmalade may seem remote, but there is a link and a rather charming one too. In the olden days, toasted bread and spices were added to the wine to give it flavour. One day some drinker with a turn for gallantry declared that a certain fair lady herself gave sufficient flavour to his wine: she was his 'toast'. The idea caught on, and the word came into general use for drinking to someone's health and happiness.

Proposing a toast involves making a speech in honour of the chosen person. Today such a speech may last only a minute or two or it may be an address of half an hour or more. There is often a speech in reply to the toast and this may be more important than the proposer's speech. An example of this is the Prime Minister's annual reply to the toast of Her Majesty's ministers at the Lord Mayor's banquet in the City of London, which becomes a wide-ranging report on the state of the nation.

If you are asked to propose a toast, begin by making sure what is expected of you. Are you being asked for 'a few well-chosen words' as a preliminary to the toast which, as at a wedding, is the really important thing, or is the invitation really a way of asking you to make an after-dinner speech? If it is the latter, then you must bear in mind that the company expect a strong element of entertainment to be mixed with anything more substantial which you have to tell them. Most frequently, the guests have enjoyed an ample meal and are relaxing in the happy afterglow of good food and wine; they are not in the mood for following complex arguments and while serious, even solemn, points may be made, these must be leavened with lighter passages and the guests eventually brought to their feet for the toast in a happy frame of mind.

Although we regard weddings as family occasions, a hundred or more guests may well be present. This is a sizeable audience, for whom a few impromptu remarks will not suffice. One hopes that every aspect of the wedding day will contribute to a memory of happiness that the bride and groom will cherish all their lives. You therefore have a responsibility, as proposer of the health of the happy couple, to do or say nothing that will cause disappointment or embarrassment to those present, as you voice the feelings of all in wishing good fortune to the newly-weds. Your speech should be prepared and rehearsed with the greatest care; it should be well spoken and it should be short. It is an unfortunate fact that all too often the 'old friend of the family' who has been asked to propose the toast turns out to be a bit of a bore, and if he launches forth on what he remembers about the bride when she was a baby, the smile on her face is apt to become fixed and glassy. Remember that the most important moment is when all present raise their glasses and wish health and happiness to the bride and the groom – your words are only a gracious preliminary. It would be appropriate for you to express your happiness at being asked to propose the toast. You should pay graceful compliments to the bride on her personal appearance as well as on her character, which you have seen develop since childhood and also praise the groom whom you have come to know more recently, for his fine qualities. You then express, on behalf of the company the warmest good wishes for their future together and ask the guests to rise and drink to the health and future happiness of the bride and the groom.

The reply to this toast is made by the bridegroom, speaking on behalf of his wife as well. His speech is usually very short. In it he should express his thanks for the toast and the kind remarks that preceded it, his happiness in having married the girl of his choice and his confidence in their future together. He should include a complimentary reference to the bride's parents and – by tradition – he should conclude by proposing the health of the bridesmaids.

They are not put to the trouble of replying to this toast, since it falls to the best man to reply on their behalf. Usually he compliments them on their appearance and on the manner in which they have carried out their duties and thanks the bridegroom for the toast just drunk. Only a very few sentences are needed for this reply and often the best man will go on to read telegrams and other messages sent by those unable to be at the reception.

If you were proposing the toast at a wedding anniversary – for example, a silver, ruby or golden wedding – you would allude to the many happy years the couple had spent together, their mutual support in times of trouble and their happiness in having their children, grandchildren and friends with them at this time. Of course the speaker must be tactful, avoiding anything which is not a matter for rejoicing, and concentrating on the things for which the couple and the family can feel genuinely grateful. The toast would conclude with the wish that they may have many more years of happiness together.

The quality of tact is most important when proposing toasts. Essentially you are praising someone and wishing him or her well. There will inevitably be sides to people's natures which are less than admirable; there will be episodes which they would prefer to forget and which they certainly do not wish the guests to be reminded of. What may seem a funny story to you may cause embarrassment or even offence to the subject of it and, by telling it, you may ruin what was intended to be a speech in his praise. Be sensitive, too, to other people present: it is possible that by over-praising the guest of honour you may seem by implication, to be criticizing other family members or colleagues. To say at a man's retirement ceremony that he virtually ran the office single-handed is a slap in the face for those who worked with him, and to say he is irreplaceable is unfair to his successor, who may well be present.

Speeches on a colleague's retirement can be delicate affairs and you should be very sensitive to the mixed feelings the occasion is bound to arouse. It should not be assumed too readily by a younger person that a man or woman relishes the idea of retiring. Many people look forward to it eagerly and cannot wait to be released from the strain of daily travel to and from work and the routine of their profession, but for others there is a sense of being unwanted, of the best part of their life being behind them and the companionship of the office or factory being henceforth closed to them. They will want to put a brave face on it and boast about the leisured life that lies ahead, but in their hearts there may be fear of empty hours which they do not know how to fill. Bear all this in mind when you plan your speech in honour of your colleague. You will almost certainly know whether he or she welcomes the change in life and you should be able to frame your speech accordingly. Make sure that a warm expression of thanks is given for all that your colleague has achieved for the organization; let him go away knowing that his work has been noticed and genuinely appreciated. Pay tribute not only to his professional skill but also to his personal qualities as a member of the team and as a friend and companion to those he has worked with and to younger colleagues whom he has helped. Avoid any suggestion that he is a 'has-been'; make him feel that right up to this moment he has played a valuable part in making the organization what it is today. In wishing him well for the future, remember to include his wife and family in your remarks if this is appropriate.

A reply to such a toast will depend very much on the attitude you take to your retirement and on your view of the firm. It has been known for a person on the point of leaving to feel that at last he can have his say and utter a few home truths which he has been biting back for thirty years. Whatever momentary satisfaction this may bring to an embittered person, it is bound to sour an occasion which was intended to be a pleasant one. If you have refrained from saying these things for thirty years, there can be little point in saying them now.

Do not allow yourself, either, to survey in detail the events of a long career; it is self-indulgent, and of more interest to the speaker than to others. Your principal theme should be thanks to your colleagues for their good wishes and farewell gifts. You should include words of appreciation for the management and the friends you have worked with, pride in the success of the organization and good wishes for its future. Like the toast itself, the speech should be warm, appreciative and quite short.

A variant on the speeches for a retirement are those made when a colleague is leaving the firm for promotion. In proposing the toast, the speaker would talk of the excellent work his colleague has done, the qualities which made promotion inevitable, and the loss, both professional and personal, which will be felt by all present. Finally there would be expressions of confidence in his future success, coupled with good wishes for his developing career. The reply would be on the lines suggested above for someone leaving the firm on retirement.

24 Debating

One's first introduction to public speaking is often as a member of a school debating society. Here the newcomers marvel at the wit and eloquence of their seniors tackling the important issues of the day. In time they themselves screw up sufficient courage to rise to their feet and make their maiden speeches. Not all debates are on serious topics; there may also be 'balloon' debates, deciding which famous character (impersonated by one of the speakers) should be thrown out of the balloon to lighten its load, or impromptu debates where the speakers are given no time at all to prepare their speeches for or against the motion. All this is great fun and also good training for the less sheltered areas of debating in the world beyond school.

At the centre of our national life are the debates in Parliament where, as we know from broadcasts, the noisy and at times unruly atmosphere of a political debating club is the froth on the surface of deliberations which affect the whole life of the nation. Its rules of debate have been established over the centuries and in the Commons are assiduously preserved by the authority of the Speaker in his chair with the mace – symbol of the rights and privileges of the Commons – on the table before him. With similar dignity the Lord Chancellor presides in the House of Lords.

Between the two extremes of school and Parliament lie many other situations where debating is the method by which issues are explored and decisions taken. University debating societies, and especially the famous Oxford and Cambridge Unions, are seen as the cradles of those who intend to make their mark in public life. When school and college are behind them, they are ready for their first taste of the real thing, whether it be the arguing out of problems in business meetings and conferences or taking their first steps into public life by seeking election to local councils.

The conduct of trials in the law courts also takes the form of a debate, with counsel on each side presenting his case, supported by the evidence of witnesses; public inquiries, for example into the routing of motorways, proceed by a form of debate; and questions of general social interest are pursued in public meetings. A much wider audience shares such events when they are broadcast on radio and television. All in all, debates play a major part in our conduct of affairs and many public speakers will have the opportunity to display their skills in this medium.

Essentially a debate is a situation where two sides of a case are argued under strict rules of procedure with the intention of persuading those present to support one side or the other. The matter to be discussed is known as the 'motion' and, as in Parliament, those present are often referred to as 'this house'. The chairman opens the proceedings with an announcement of the motion. He will say something along these lines: 'The motion for debate is that in the opinion of this house all experiments on animals should be abandoned forthwith.' He may then announce the names of the principal speakers before calling on the proposer to open the debate.

The proposer is followed by the opposer. Each will have a seconder and in some debates there will be other members of their teams who will speak third or even fourth on each side.

A debater's task is to present his case in the most favourable light possible. Although he may recognize that there is much to be said for some part of his opponent's case, he will not admit this, except as a tactical ploy to earn a reputation for reasonableness which will gain him sympathy and respect when he goes on to demolish the rest of the opposition's arguments. The proposer of the motion has the privilege and the disadvantage of speaking first. The privilege lies in the fact that he can choose the battleground, set out the problem as he sees it and make the initial impact on the minds of the audience. The disadvantage is that he does not know the line which the opposition will take and, by declaring his hand, will lay himself open to attack by subsequent speakers unless he is skilful enough to anticipate every possible move by his opponents.

The opposer, like all the other speakers, will be taking notes on what is being said. When he rises to make his opening speech, he has to capture the initiative from the proposer. One way is to redefine the motion so that the emphasis falls on aspects more favourable to his side – shifting the battleground, as it were. Another way is to tackle head on and refute some of the chief points the proposer has just made. When exactly to do this must be a matter of judgement. Some opposers will begin straight away disposing of the proposer's arguments and, having done so, proceed with their prepared speeches. Others will prefer to use the opening they have carefully planned, not wishing to weaken its effect by preceding it with impromptu comments on the proposer. Usually this is preferable; use your prepared opening and then deal briefly with your opponent's points. Once you have done this, you can go on with presenting the case for your own side.

All the speakers in a debate will be expected to conform to the time limit allocated to them. The longest times will be granted to the proposer and the opposer: fifteen minutes might be the rule for them. Then their seconders would be allowed no more than ten minutes and speakers from the floor only five.

Those who speak second or third in a debating team will have discussed tactics beforehand with their principals and decided on the line they are to take. The proposer or opposer will agree to leave them two or three points that will reinforce the main ones that have already been used. But the second and third speakers will have to be ready to move from their prepared notes and reply impromptu to the points that their opponents have made in earlier speeches. This calls for quick wit, a ready turn of phrase and the shrewdness to exploit a weakness that can be detected in the opposition's arguments. If the proposer and the opposer are the big guns in the debate, then the seconders are the skirmishing light cavalry.

When all the principal speakers have had their say, the chairman will throw the debate open to 'the floor of the house', and any member present can now stand up in the hope that the chairman will give him the opportunity to speak; it is the chairman's duty to allow as many to speak as time will permit. Speakers from the floor are unlikely to have prepared their remarks in advance. Usually they respond to some point that has been made, either supporting or opposing it, in a short impromptu speech. Often this will conclude with some such phrase as 'I therefore call on the house to support (or oppose) the motion', though this is not obligatory.

At the end of the debate, the proposer, who up to now has not been able to comment on what has been said, is given five minutes to reply to the debate. Some societies also allow the opposer a winding-up speech, which would come before that of the proposer, who always has the last word. After this all discussion is at an end; the chairman reads out the motion again and puts it to the vote, and the motion is then declared to be carried or defeated.

A debate differs from a discussion in that interruption of a speaker is very severely limited. While applause and laughter are of course permitted, no one may intervene in a speech except under the rules laid down, usually only on points of order or explanation. A point of order occurs when a member feels that one of the rules of the society has been breached, and the chairman will, if he agrees, ask the speaker to put the matter right by apologizing or rephrasing his remarks. Sometimes, too, the speaker has to be corrected because he has misunderstood what has been said. Such interventions can be made only with the chairman's permission, the person wishing to intervene having drawn attention to himself by standing up. If the chairman calls on him to make his point, then the original speaker must sit down, for only one speaker may be on his feet at a time.

This rule, like all the others in a formal debate, is intended to maintain good order and civilized behaviour. To this end, no one ever addresses another member directly; all remarks are addressed to the chairman, who on the first occasion is called by the speaker 'Mr (or Madam) Chairman' and thereafter 'sir' or 'madam'. When a speaker wishes to talk about the remarks made by another person present, he uses such phrases as 'the previous speaker' or 'the member who spoke a few moments ago' and his comments are addressed via the chairman. Should a speaker inadvertently speak directly to and name another member, most of the house would rise to draw attention to this lapse on a point of order.

25 Speaking extempore

The best advice about extempore speaking might be, 'Don't do it!' It is flying in the face of all that has been said in this book hitherto to suggest that you can rise to your feet at a moment's notice and deliver a well-rounded speech with no preparation at all. Yet there are virtuoso performers with nimble wits, enviable fluency and wide experience who can hold an audience spellbound with a full-length extempore speech – when the visiting speaker has been taken ill suddenly, perhaps, or thick fog makes his arrival that night highly unlikely.

More common is the situation when you are asked to speak briefly off the cuff in connection with business or local affairs. The essence of the situation is its unexpectedness. One minute you are sitting back at a meeting, listening to the discussion, and the next the chairman has turned to you with an encouraging smile, saying, 'I'm sure Mr X would say a few words about his own experience of this problem.' There are murmurs of assent, possibly a small round of applause and you stand up, having been instantly transformed from a happy member of the listening group into an apprehensive public speaker. Let us say you had come to the meeting to hear speeches from county officials on building a bypass around your town. In the discussion that followed someone referred to the effect on businesses in the High Street. Your shop was mentioned and the chairman has called on you for your comments. You came to the meeting only to listen; now you have to speak – extempore!

It is easy to think of similar situations – you are called upon to make a spontaneous toast to a colleague who has unexpectedly announced his engagement or a vote of thanks about which the chairman (unforgivably) did not warn you in advance, or you might be asked to explain the background of a situation under discussion because some people seem less well informed than was assumed.

There are two helpful rules. The first is: keep to the point. There must have been a very definite reason for your being invited to speak without previous warning, as in the examples given above. Do not waste time on preliminaries. No one is expecting you to produce an elaborate introduction and you certainly do not have the time to think of one. Go straight to the point, stating it clearly and simply. As you develop your views, interesting digressions from your main point may occur to you. Rapidly assess if they are going to be helpful in extending the argument or if they are merely going to complicate matters; it is very likely that in pursuing any deviations from the main line of your argument you will end up by confusing the audience and losing the thread of your own remarks. If you do decide to embark on a side-issue, be sure you know how to relate it to your principal theme in such a way that you can return to the main line of your argument without difficulty.

The second rule of extempore speaking is: keep it brief. A danger in inviting someone 'to say a few words' is that once he has the floor to himself he will go on and on . . . and on! Remember: extempore speaking is no excuse for rambling. It is quite extraordinary how some speakers lose all sense of time. Before being asked to speak, they would say that speaking extempore terrifies them, but once the opportunity occurs, it seems that nothing can hold them. They discover an unexpected fluency (of a kind) and threaten to become unstoppable. What is more, such people become quite impervious to yawns and fidgets around them or else they notice them and remark cheerily, 'I know I'm going on a bit, but I must tell you . . .' and they are off again with renewed vigour. The effective extempore speech will be a short one: keep to the point and keep it brief.

26 Making announcements

'I'm afraid there is a mistake in your programmes. Tea will not be served at five o'clock in the marquee, but at four o'clock on the lawn behind the flower tent.'

No problem about making simple announcements such as that, surely? Certainly not, if they were all as straightforward and if the announcer took pains to speak them slowly and clearly. But only too often the wording is muddled or the diction indistinct, causing confusion and misunderstanding.

We have to listen to announcements far more often than we might suspect. Important notices from the authorities – about traffic conditions for example – come over the radio and TV every day. Government announcements come as part of the news programmes on the media and programme presenters on the national and local radio frequently insert notices of forthcoming events or of competitions they are running. These announcements, presented by professionals, are usually clear, succinct and, of course, audible. But this is not always the case when ordinary mortals find themselves asked by a harassed vicar at a garden fête to announce that someone's car is blocking him in or when a businessman has to start the day briefing his team or the secretary of a social club has to announce details of forthcoming events. Whether they realize it or not, all these people are public speakers and the ability to make announcements in such a way that they can be easily understood and acted on is something that everyone in such a position should cultivate.

As always, preparation is important. To scribble a scrap of information on the back of an envelope and then, an hour later, drag it from your pocket in front of an audience and try to make sense of it is asking for trouble. If it is your job as chairman or secretary of an organization to make announcements at a meeting, then ten minutes spent putting the notices in order beforehand will be time very well spent. It will be best to write down what you are going to say and read it out – it is not like a complete speech, where an impression of spontaneity is required. Most notices involve a time and a place, and it is worth repeating these at the end of your announcement. Keep the wording simple and the facts clear, and avoid any personal asides that may distract the listener.

Be sure too that when you come to the announcements you have the attention of your audience. If there has been a break in the meeting and a buzz of conversation has developed, do not begin giving out the notices until the audience are once again ready to listen to you. Some convenient and courteous phrase such as, 'May I have your attention, please?' will be enough to restore order and ensure that everyone is listening.

Audiences like to know how long they are going to be asked to concentrate, so it is a good idea to warn them if you have several things for them to take in. Use an introductory remark such as, 'I have a long list of announcements for you this evening, so I must ask you to be patient with me.' The audience will then subconsciously adjust to a period for notices which will be longer than usual. On the other hand, you can also alert them to the fact that there are to be only one or two notices to be given out, with the implication that they had better be awake or they will have missed them!

Notices are often very short – and usually all the better for that – so you need to be sure that the point has gone across satisfactorily. An unfortunately timed cough or the slamming of a door can easily blot out the really vital piece of information. Do not sweep on to the next announcement regardless of the interruption: go over whatever part of the notice has been obscured and, by means of eye-contact, assure yourself that what you have read out has been heard and (as far as you can tell) understood.

Finally, it is often a good idea to pin up a list of the announcements where they can be consulted later by those interested. People sometimes want to verify the details or copy down dates, etc., in their diaries which were not to hand when you were speaking. Typing out your notices beforehand makes them easy for you to read and afterwards you can pin this sheet to a notice-board.

27 Reading the minutes
   — and more

It may seem surprising to include a chapter on reading aloud in a book on public speaking. It certainly has nothing to do with reading your speech, which is something to be done only in very exceptional circumstances. Yet there are times when public speakers are called on to read their own or other people's writings. The most obvious example of this is the task of the secretary of an organization. At every meeting he will have to read the minutes of the previous meeting, though the cry, 'Take them as read,' may ring out as soon as he stands up – to the relief of the secretary himself and of all present. This may be due to a desire to get on with the main events of the evening and not drag through details of what happened weeks before, but some of the blame may rest with a secretary whose organizational abilities outstrip his skill as a reader.

This is a pity, because it is not only the minutes that have to be read aloud. Sometimes correspondence has to be put before a meeting and read effectively so that its implications can be considered. In business circles, a speaker may have to present a report, the wording of which must be so carefully judged that it has to be written out in full. Representatives of firms and trade unions have to read out prepared statements to the press. At political meetings declarations of policy may have to be quoted in precise terms, which will involve reading aloud from a written text. All these are examples where public speakers need to know something of the neglected art of reading aloud.

Quite often a public speaker will want to illustrate a point by reading an extract from a book or an article, and it is by no means unknown for an otherwise lively speaker to become boring and ineffective when he reads someone else's words from a written text. But this is the very passage he has chosen to clinch his argument! He too needs to heed some advice on how to read aloud.

We sometimes assume that certain people are good readers by nature, while the rest of us can opt out by saying, 'I'm just no good at it.' The truth is that most of us have not stopped to think what is involved in effective reading nor have we practised to acquire the necessary skill. Reading aloud will certainly come more easily to some than to others, but there is a great deal that most of us can do to improve our performance.

Reading aloud involves two basic activities – comprehension and interpretation. It sounds obvious to say so, but you have to understand the meaning before you can read it aloud effectively. If you have time to prepare your reading, as is desirable, this is unlikely to be a problem, but if you are called on to read at sight then natural quickness at understanding what is written will stand you in good stead. If you always need time to take in a written text, then – until you have practised to increase your skill – you would do better to arrange for someone else to do any sight-reading for you. However, there are one or two tips to help you in an emergency, which will be mentioned later.

Once you comprehend the meaning of your text, your task is then to interpret it – that is, change it into vocal sound so that it comes alive for your listeners and holds their attention. You cannot make it sound like ordinary speech, for the simple reason that it is not ordinary speech! The written language differs considerably from the spoken and this fact is not always well understood. Written English is more precise, more carefully weighed and more objective than its spoken counterpart; it will usually be more formal and structured. When you read it aloud, it will be instantly recognized as written rather than spoken language.

Being a reader you have to take account of these facts, and at the same time, you have to give the passage life, so that the audience will be alert and interested and not simply longing for you to finish reading and become human again.

As with all other speech activities, you have to prepare and rehearse for the best results. When a musician practises, he has a pencil by him and he adds all sorts of additional markings to the printed music – fingerings, phrase marks, dynamics and so on. In the same way, if you have an important piece of reading to do – and even the minutes of the previous meeting have their importance – then you, too, might find it helpful to add markings to the text to enable you to read more effectively and with more confidence.

The flow of words on the printed page has already been marked off in units by the punctuation and this is the first prop for the reader. It is amazing how many people take no notice of commas when they read aloud, and even full stops may be skated over and treated as if they did not exist. These punctuation marks assist the reader in assimilating the text, showing where he must pause momentarily as he reads to himself. How much more useful are they to those of us who must read aloud, if only we would accept the help they offer! One of the first things you might do with your pencil is to put a circle around the full stops, just to remind yourself of the natural stopping places the writer has put in for you. Circle any semicolons too. They act like small full stops, separating the main ideas within a sentence. Time and again one hears the semicolon being treated like an unimportant comma as the reader sweeps over it, but it should always be used to mark a significant pause.

So far you have used your pencil only to draw attention to the existing punctuation. But there is more to do. Sometimes the writer has created long phrases without commas that would be easier to read if they were broken up. In such cases, add the commas or breath marks of your own. (A large **V** is a helpful conventional sign for a breath.) Of course you do not need to take a breath at every comma; for most you will need the slightest of pauses and then you continue in the same breath. You will find that most sentences of average length can be done in one breath. But if the sentence is rather long, you can decide for yourself where is the best place to take a breath and you should mark it accordingly.

Monotony is the great enemy of effective reading aloud and it is caused by delivering everything at one low level and at one unvarying speed. Therefore lightly underline with your pencil the important words in a sentence as a reminder that these will need special emphasis. It is quite remarkable how this simple device improves the expressiveness of your reading.

Here is an extract from the minutes of a staff–parents meeting at a comprehensive school, with some suggested markings. Practise reading this aloud, giving full value to the markings. Then study the second extract and decide for yourself where you should mark it. (You might like to tape-record this passage without any special preparation and then record it again when you have marked it up. You should hear a distinct improvement.)

SCHOOL BUSES

Mrs Hunton, the mother of a <u>first</u>-year child, complained of the behaviour of <u>senior</u> pupils on the bus which served her village of Kennon. There was <u>smoking</u> and <u>bad language</u>, and younger pupils were forced to give up their seats so that the <u>older</u> ones could sit together. There seemed to be no <u>discipline</u> on the buses **V** and she understood that the bus driver had <u>also</u> complained to the school. She wanted to know if <u>other</u> parents shared her feelings about this problem and what action was to be taken by the <u>staff</u>.

<u>Several</u> other parents with children living in Kennon voiced their <u>support</u>, **V** although <u>Mr Johnson</u>, whose son was in the <u>fifth</u> form, remarked that these complaints arose <u>every</u> year when new pupils began to find their feet in the school. They should understand that senior pupils had the <u>right</u> to sit with their friends **V** and he believed that the accusations over smoking and swearing were based on <u>isolated</u> incidents only.

In his reply, the Headmaster said that while he agreed with the previous speaker that the incidents were probably <u>isolated</u>, parents of young pupils were <u>genuinely concerned</u>. He would <u>not</u> tolerate bad behaviour on school buses **V** and so he was appointing sixth formers as bus prefects **V** who would report to him every day <u>any</u> misbehaviour. He would be taking <u>firm action</u> against offenders.

THE LIBRARY

The School Librarian, Miss Joslin, announced to the meeting that plans for an extension to the school library had been accepted by the governors and the Local Education Authority and she asked for the support of the meeting in raising money to purchase books for the new section of the library which would be devoted to science subjects, at present badly represented in the collection. She

explained that the LEA would fund the erection of the
new building, which would be linked to the existing
building with a covered way, but they would not be able
to provide extra money for new books. She was appealing
to the parents and staff members of the committee to
undertake the organization of fund-raising activities in
the next six months, so that when the building was complete there would be enough new science books to fill the
shelves.

The chairman welcomed this new development in the
school's building scheme and said he felt sure all members present would be eager to help in the provision of
books.

When you have studied your text and marked it up, you must
rehearse it and in due course deliver it to an audience. Beyond any
doubt, what the audience will be most grateful for is sheer audibility.
As in all aspects of public speaking, think of the people in the back
row and direct your voice towards them. Nothing is more irritating
than to half-hear what is being said or read out. Sheer volume is not
enough either. What is also required is sharp, clean diction, with
the vowel sounds well formed and the consonants in place. A loud
voice is not necessarily a clear voice and if the diction is poor, a loud
voice becomes just an annoying boom. A light, well-produced voice
with excellent diction will carry further than a noisy blur of indistinct syllables.

Assuming that you can be heard clearly, you then have to concentrate on making even a seemingly dull piece of writing interesting
to your audience. A good deal will depend on your own attitude. If
you say to yourself, in effect, 'Somebody else wrote this; the words
are his responsibility, not mine. I'm just a voice,' you are heading
straight down the road to boredom. The more productive approach
is to say, 'I want to tell this to the audience because both the author
and I think it worth hearing. I want the audience to share this with
us and I'm going to do all I can to put it over well.'

So what is going to prevent your reading from being a success? Next
to inaudibility itself, the chief fault is choosing *too fast a pace*. 'Slow
up, slow up,' one longs to cry out to the inexperienced reader. The

words pour out, the pauses are ignored and the meaning is lost in a cascade of words.

Training yourself to adopt a suitable pace is not easy. Nerves make us want to move on and even when we think we have chosen the right speed, we can find ourselves hurrying away without being aware of it. Practice with an honest and helpfully critical friend is useful, but a tape-recorder is likely to be more readily available. The only warning here is that you should not speak confidentially into the microphone as if it were a telephone. Stand some distance away from it and imagine you are reading your report in a large room, to some extent simulating the conditions under which you will eventually have to read. If the recording shows you to be guilty of reading too fast, then try again, adopting a slower pace and pausing at every full stop for rather longer than you did before. Failure to make use of natural pauses gives the impression of relentless speed.

Of course some readers – the minority – have a tendency to go to the opposite extreme and read too slowly. One way of improving this fault is to be quite certain that you are reading phrases and not single words. Look a few words ahead – say, up to the next comma or breath mark – and deliver this in a smooth speech rhythm, and then add the next phrase or phrases up to the end of the sentence.

The ability to read a few words ahead is an essential for all readers, swift or slow. Only by knowing what is coming can you take the necessary breath, adopt the appropriate intonation and manage the phrase or sentence correctly. It is an art that comes with practice and is not too difficult to acquire, providing you are not reading too quickly. You can practise this straight away by reading aloud the previous paragraph of this chapter. Before you say a word, read the whole paragraph again to be sure you know its drift. Then prepare to read aloud. Do not speak until you have read and quickly memorized the first six words ('Of course some readers – the minority . . .'). Then begin to read aloud by saying these words *without looking at them*, while your eye is taking in the words 'have a tendency to go to the opposite extreme'. As you speak that phrase, your eye should be registering 'and read too slowly'. Then comes a full stop. Use it! The slight pause at that point will allow you time to take in the words 'One way of improving this fault', so that when you begin the second sentence, your eye will be on 'is to be quite certain that you are reading phrases'.

You can now read on, practising the same technique. You will be surprised how quickly you pick up the skill and, as it develops, you can lengthen the units which you can memorize. But remember that your best friend is the full stop or semicolon, which affords you that natural resting point from which you can start again. Obviously this is not meant to suggest that a lengthy pause is introduced at every full stop. It will only be a second or so in length, but this will be quite sufficient to mark the end of the sentence for your listeners and enable you to glance ahead.

At the end of paragraphs you should make a more substantial pause than at the end of sentences. Your listeners should be clearly aware that one section of the reading has ended and that a different topic or aspect of the matter is about to be presented.

Having got the pace right, how can you go about bringing *variety* into your reading? If everything is delivered in absolutely the same way from the beginning to the end of the paragraph, boredom will set in and you will have deserved the glazed looks and uncomfortable shufflings. To avoid these, pay attention to the variables of pace, pitch and intonation

If you have been at pains to bring your too-rapid delivery down to a suitable rate, you may feel uneasy at being told that there are occasions when you might speed it up again. Yet a change of pace is one element of the variety that experienced readers use. An aside in the writing, a quip or a short illustration may warrant a slight increase in speed. Then you can pointedly slow up afterwards when you return to the main theme.

Very effective indeed is a marked slowing of pace. This would be used when you came to a really important remark that you wanted everyone to consider very carefully. Your sudden change, accompanied by suitable emphasis on the appropriate words, would have a considerable effect on the audience. This would be the sort of place to mark with your pencil when you are preparing the text. You should not leave an effect like this to chance.

Variation of the pitch of the voice is another effect that an experienced reader will use. While nerves may induce a rather high pitch in some people, most beginners are likely to pitch their voices too low when they read aloud. If you are aware that this could apply to you – or if it is revealed to you by your critical friends or your objective tape-recorder – then practise raising the pitch a tone or two into the middle of your speech range. Few of us make much use of the very wide range of pitch which nature has granted to us. Just think of the vocal range available to us, rising from that miserable grunt deep in the middle of the chest when we complain about having to get up in the morning to the high shriek we are capable of if suddenly frightened. Yet in normal speech we use only a very narrow band of tones, and when we read aloud these seem to become even more restricted.

What so often happens to an inexperienced reader is that, having made a good start by raising the pitch of his voice, he then progressively drops it until it reaches rock bottom – and there it stays. This comes about from a natural characteristic of our English speech. Unless you are asking a certain kind of question, the tune of the voice falls as it moves towards the end of a sentence, thereby lowering the pitch. The reader is then tempted to begin the next sentence *at that same low pitch*. The level will drop even further at the end of that sentence and so on, until (within as little as two or three sentences) the lowest pitch has been reached and there it remains!

There is one sure way to avoid this: begin the first sentence at a reasonable middle pitch of the voice and then return to this pitch at the start of every new sentence. This advice is so simple, yet new readers find it very difficult to achieve. Obviously it needs practice. Once you have acquired this skill, you should have enough flexibility to choose a slightly different pitch for each new sentence: some may be lower than your norm, others higher. You will make your choice of whatever seems the most expressive for that sentence.

The third variable which gives interest and life to your reading is intonation – the tunes of speech, conveyed by the subtle rise and fall of the voice. The tunes are very complex. In ordinary speech we use them with remarkable skill to convey nuances of meaning and feeling that simply cannot be conveyed by the written word. When we read aloud, we should imagine the voice of the writer and try to convey something of the speech tunes he would have used if he were speaking directly to us. We can be sure that if he were trying to interest his listeners, he would not use a flat monotone. Therefore the rise and fall of normal speech tunes should be deployed, or even heightened, to make the desired effect in a large hall.

Passages involving dialogue require additional skills, not yet mentioned. Teachers reading to children and clergy and lay people reading in churches would have to meet this challenge. Inverted commas on a page are signals to the reader that something special is required of him. The author is recording the actual words of a person in his story and the reader has to respond by characterizing that person with his voice: for a few seconds he has to become an actor, giving the intonation and expression to the quoted words that are appropriate to the character. The more level delivery of the narrative section is enlivened by the introduction of these elements of spoken English, giving variety to the reading.

Another valuable technique is the use of pause. You can imagine the effect on an audience if, in the middle of a long passage, the reader suddenly stops dead. Every head in the audience jerks up, a sudden chill falls on the room and everyone is alert and expectant. This is an extreme example of the effect of pause – if you need to stir a somnolent audience like this, you have not been doing a very good job! But there is no doubt that a pause does command attention. It should be used sparingly, for repetition rapidly dulls any effect, and it has to be in the right place. It is particularly useful in drawing attention to an important word or phrase. Just before you utter it, insert a short pause and at once the audience is held momentarily in suspense as to what is coming next; they are thus subconsciously prepared to give it special attention. Try saying the following sentence in two ways: (a) smoothly and without any break and (b) with a short but distinct pause before the word 'disaster'.

(a) What we find ourselves facing is disaster.
(b) What we find ourselves facing is – disaster.

You will find that in sentence (b) the word 'disaster' becomes much more dramatic and impressive than in (a).

A pause is also useful before an important remark, perhaps one which sums up what has already been argued or one which gives a decision for which the audience has been waiting. As has been said earlier, every full stop requires at least a brief pause and at the end of the paragraph the pause should be very definite indeed.

As in all forms of speaking before an audience, there is more to reading aloud than simply using your voice skilfully. You also communicate with your whole body. Stance is important, the way you hold your book is important – and the use you make of your eyes is very important indeed. Your stance will often be determined by the way you are using your script.

If you place it on a flat table and attempt to read it from there, you will inevitably be stooping over it; if you hold it too low, your head will be down as you read and your voice will be directed at the floor instead of to the back of the hall. On the other hand, if you hold it too high, you will obscure your face and again to some extent block off your voice. The ideal is to hold the script in a comfortable position at about chest level and some way out in front of you. This will enable you to stand up well and face the audience with the script in an excellent position for you to see it, but without allowing it to become an obstacle to communication. You will look right and you will sound right.

There is an old saying that the eyes are the windows of the soul. Too many readers forget this – they keep their eyes glued to the script and never once lift them to their listeners. Yet a reading is transformed when the reader from time to time raises his eyes and looks at his audience. Beginners are often afraid to look up because they feel that once they look up from the script they will lose their place and never be able to recover. To overcome this, there is no need to run your finger along the line like a child learning to read, but it does help if you keep a thumb at the level of the line you are reading and gently slide it down the margin as you read. Then you can look up with some confidence, knowing that your helpful thumb will take you back to the line where you risked leaving the safety of the printed word.

There is a technique which helps you to look up from the text with confidence, related to the ability to read several words ahead which was mentioned earlier. The obvious place to raise your eyes is towards the end of a sentence – not necessarily every time, but quite often in the course of one paragraph. It works like this: reading half a line or more ahead (as already explained) you see the full stop approaching; despite every psychological pull to the contrary, you force yourself to raise your eyes to the audience, speaking those last words from memory and resisting every temptation to drop them until you reach the full stop. Only then do you permit yourself to look down and read the next half line and so begin again. The inexperienced reader panics at this advice, believing he must desperately read at least the beginning of the next sentence while concluding the present one. What he is forgetting is that there is a natural pause at every full stop and, brief though it is, this pause is quite long enough for him to find his place again in the text and prepare to read the following sentence. Moreover, the very act of stopping to prepare the next sentence automatically makes the reader pause at the full stop, thus avoiding the rushed delivery that so often mars a reading.

All this comes with practice. Once you have some confidence in raising your eyes as the full stop approaches, you will find that sometimes it is also possible and desirable to raise your eyes to the audience part way through a sentence, at a comma for instance, especially if the sentence is a long one. With this sort of eye-contact, you will find that you are not simply in touch with your audience but are actually in command of them, compelling their attention not only with your voice but with the force of your personality, conveyed through your eyes.

Sight-reading

All that has been said so far assumes that the person reading aloud has had time to study and rehearse his script. But there are occasions when something is thrust upon us and we have to sight-read. It is unlikely that you will have no time at all to prepare. You may have as much as five or ten minutes, which under the circumstances is quite a substantial time, in which much can be done. But what can you do if you have only ten seconds?

The essential thing is to discover the nature of what you have to read. A quick glance over the first few lines should tell you this. Another quick glance will tell you the length of your assignment and therefore how you will have to pace your reading. This rapid inspection of the text will also give you an idea of the style – whether the sentences are long or short; whether there is dialogue; whether the writer is using technical jargon or other specialized vocabulary which may present a problem. If you really have as little as ten seconds before you have to read, these discoveries will serve to do little more than alert you to possible difficulties ahead. There is nothing else for it: you must take a good breath and begin.

The advice about reading ahead, given earlier in this section, is of prime importance in sight-reading. You need to be aware how far away the first comma is and then the first full stop. Here, as already explained, you can pause and readjust for the next sentence – and so on to the end of the paragraph, when a substantial pause is required. Try, too, to anticipate where the key words of each sentence are, so that you can given them special emphasis when you come to them. You have had no time to underline them with pencil, but you must be ready to give them the weight that their importance demands.

As always, avoid haste in your sight-reading. Considering how much you have to do on the spur of the moment it would be folly to set yourself such a cracking pace that the first long word or unexpected piece of phrasing sends you sprawling. In any case, fast reading is the enemy of expressiveness, and with sight-reading it is simply asking for trouble.

5   Organizing a Meeting

28   Organizing a speaker

Your career as a public speaker begins the moment the telephone rings and a voice at the other end invites you to come to a meeting and deliver a talk for the first time. For the purpose of this chapter, let us leave you at your end of the telephone and go down the line to where the organizer of the event is phoning you. What should he be saying to you and, if he does not say it, what should you be asking him?

The organizer of an event will have a great many things to see to – booking the hall, advertising the event, circulating his members, perhaps arranging for refreshments and planning the whole programme for the evening. If he is in charge of a large formal dinner, he will be busy with the hotel management or the caterers, the florist, possibly also musicians and entertainers, as well as the guest speakers. We shall concentrate on this last item on his long list and look at things from his point of view. Better still, let us assume that you have been asked to organize an event and book a speaker. How should you go about it?

You begin by writing or phoning the speaker of your choice and inviting him to address your meeting. Phoning is the better method because you get an instant response and can exchange a great deal of necessary information freely and informally. Confirmation by letter can follow.

There are certain basic facts a speaker needs to know. First of all, you should identify yourself and give the name of your organization and your position within it. Mention any contact, such as a mutual acquaintance who has recommened the speaker. Then issue your invitation, giving the date, time and place. All this is sufficiently obvious, but there is a good deal more to be talked about, so do not put the phone down too quickly after those essential details have been established and the invitation accepted. There are some things about the speaker that you wish to know and many that he ought to discuss with you.

First of all, you both need to be clear about the subject of the talk and, if it is to be publicized in advance (as is usual), you will want to be given a title for it. You may wish for more information about the speaker himself, his background and qualifications, which will be useful for advertising and the press release, and for the chairman's introductory remarks. The easiest way with this is to ask for the details to be sent to you in writing. You should also inquire about the speaker's method of transport, whether he knows where the hall is and how to get there. If he is uncertain of its location, then assure him you will send a map and full instructions, including advice on parking. Perhaps he is coming from a distance; you will therefore discuss hospitality with him and, if required, arrangements for over-night accommodation. An offer of a meal before the event may be very welcome to someone who will be travelling a long way. Ignoring such matters and leaving your guest to fend for himself does not make a good impression.

All these points are vital to you, the organizer, but there are many others which are equally vital to the speaker and which he expects to discuss with you. As he is probably a stranger to you and your organization, he will be happier – and more successful as a speaker – if he is told in advance as much as possible about the occasion and its circumstances. If you do not tell him, he should ask. Between the two of you, the following points should be covered:

Hall

Tell him the size of the hall, anything unusual about its layout, whether he will be on a platform or at floor level, and if there is a reading-desk of some kind or just a simple table. (You might make a mental note to yourself to check on the lighting, ensuring that there is enough to enable the speaker to read his notes without difficulty.)

Mention to him the availability or otherwise of a microphone and note his reaction. Some speakers will be pleased to use a mike; others reluctant or downright suspicious. If he is keen to use a microphone, make sure it will be ready for him. The speaker may be bringing visual aids that need to be displayed; he may even wish to show slides or a video. All this will have to be discussed, because it may involve you in providing equipment for him and a table for his exhibits.

Audience

Information about the audience is very important to a speaker. Let him know how many you expect to be present and the range of their ages and interests. Warn him if there are any sensitive political, religious or social issues that should be avoided. The speaker will be interested to know if the audience has a particular reason for wanting to hear him on his subject.

Format

It is helpful to the speaker if you tell him the pattern of your meetings. For example, you may precede his talk with a half hour of your society's business. Would this mean that he could not try out the hall for its acoustics before the meeting or that he would have to arrive quite a long time before his talk? Would he have a greenroom to wait in or would he have to sit through the first part of the meeting in the hall? Are there to be other speakers and, if so, when during the proceedings will he be called to speak? Explain to him, if he is an after-dinner speaker, the programme for the evening. Tell him the name of the chairman and the other speakers.

Questions

After a lecture, it is usual to invite the audience to ask questions. Check that your visitor agrees and – most important – tell him politely but firmly how long he is expected to speak for and how long will be allowed for the subsequent questions and answers.

Fees

The question of a fee or expenses is very important and very delicate. It is probably a good idea to raise this fairly early in the conversation, since it would be a waste of time discussing all the items mentioned above if the speaker is going to refuse the engagement because you cannot meet his fee. Perhaps your organization relies on unpaid speakers. In this case you should surely offer expenses, if only enough to cover the petrol. Tactfully broach this subject before the conversation has developed too far and if it becomes clear that you cannot secure the speaker because of your limited finances, then bring the conversation to an early close with apologies and expressions of regret for troubling him. You may be in the fortunate position of being able to ask the speaker his fee and agreeing to it whatever it is. On the other hand, your resources may be limited and the speaker himself unsure as to what he should ask. It is therefore helpful to both parties if you suggest the kind of fee you usually pay your visitors. If the speaker finds it too little, he can say so or begin to negotiate with you. There is no need for either of you to feel shamefaced about this: it is part of the business of public speaking. What *is* regrettable is for you, as organizer, to assume blithely that a potential guest speaker is willing to give a good deal of time and effort for the sake of your members without reward. The visitor may indeed be willing to do so, but you should not take this for granted. Nor should you appear offended if *he* raises the matter of a fee and/or expenses. It is you who are at fault for not dealing with this earlier.

All this could make quite a lengthy phone call, and none the worse for that. There may be a need for two conversations, especially if the booking is made several months ahead. Then some details can wait until nearer the day. These would include the precise time the speaker is expected to arrive, where exactly he should go and who will be there to meet him. At the end of the first conversation, when the booking is verbally agreed, make sure you have the speaker's address correctly and tell him you will be confirming these details in writing very shortly. Give him your name, address and phone number in case he wants to come back to you before your letter arrives. If there is a long gap between the booking and the event, make a note in your diary to contact the speaker a week or two before his visit to make sure he has not forgotten it.

29 Introducing and thanking a speaker

It normally falls to the chairman to present the speaker to the audience, though sometimes, by arrangement, another person is asked to make the introduction. Whoever undertakes the task has essentially three things to do: he must welcome the speaker and he must tell the audience who he is and what he is going to talk about.

Chairmen often make the mistake of going on too long when introducing a speaker. The audience have not come to hear the chairman but the visitor and the most effective introduction is the one that is courteous, informative – and brief! A warmly expressed welcome to the guest sets the tone for the meeting and does something to put the visitor at his ease. Then the chairman should give the audience some details of the speaker's background, concentrating on those that are most relevant to his talk. The speaker comes, one assumes, as an authority on his subject and audiences like to be told something of his qualifications and experience. If the speaker is previously unknown to him, then it is the task of the introducer to find out these details before the meeting so that he can plan an adequate welcome. It is very useful if the speaker sends the chairman a short statement of his career and qualifications in advance.

Quite often the chairman will have met the speaker previously; very possibly he has also heard him speak. If this is so, the chairman can refer to this in his introduction and add his personal testimony to the quality of their guest. He should go on to announce clearly the title of the talk and express the keen anticipation with which all present are waiting to hear it. The introduction can be rounded off with some such phrase as 'I have pleasure in calling on — to address us' or 'I ask you to welcome —.' The whole introduction should not last more than two or three minutes.

Thanking a speaker

If you are asked to propose a vote of thanks, all you have to do is say a few words of appreciation and lead the audience in a round of applause.

They will already have applauded the speaker at the end of his speech and your own remarks run the danger of being an anticlimax. They will, however, be particularly useful if the main speech has been followed by a question-and-answer session. This may have run out of steam and will be brought to a conclusion by the chairman or, if questions are still forthcoming, the chairman may have to close the meeting because of time. In each case, it falls to you to round off the occasion with a few words of thanks. Like the introduction of a speaker, your speech should be brief and to the point. The evening is over and the audience want to be on their way home; they certainly do not wish to sit through another speech of some length from you.

Although you can do a little towards planning your remarks in advance, you will be most effective if you can show your appreciation of what has actually been said. To do this you will have to be alert throughout the session, noting down anything that particularly appeals to you. This may be a strongly expressed opinion of the speaker or an experience which he described particularly vividly. Take note too of what impresses you most in the tone and manner of the speech and allude to these aspects during your remarks. Remember that you are speaking on behalf of those present and address your remarks directly to the visitor.

You may care to begin by saying how much you have learnt from the talk. You might compliment the speaker on his ability to stimulate interest, to arouse enthusiasm or to send everyone away with a great deal to think about. If you know that the speaker has travelled a long distance to address you or has fitted the meeting into a very busy schedule, then incorporate this into your expression of gratitude. Conclude by inviting the audience once more to express their appreciation of all the speaker has done for them.

Unfortunately it sometimes happens that a speech has not been a great success. Do not add to the embarrassment by lavishing praise on what everyone knows has been an indifferent performance; praise its best feature and keep your remarks brief.

30 The chairman

The chairman is himself a public speaker. He may never have occasion to give a lengthy address, but at every meeting he will be making a speech of welcome to the guest speaker and very possibly expressing thanks to the visitor at the end. He will therefore know how a speaker feels and should use this knowledge to fulfil one of his principal duties – putting the guest at his ease. He also has the responsibility of ensuring that the audience is kept happy and for this he will employ tact, humour and a degree of firmness.

Before the event he should make sure that the organizer (presumably the secretary of his organization) has briefed him fully about the visiting speaker and his talk. When he meets his guest, he should know his name and how to pronounce it. The chairman should also show that he has studied the CV sent in by the speaker or, if there is no CV, has taken the trouble to find out something about him. A warm and friendly greeting begins the process of helping the visitor to feel at ease.

The chairman should then make sure that all the arrangements are as the speaker requested. Providing that the audience have not already filled the hall, last-minute adjustments can be made to the arrangement of the platform and the setting out of exhibits, and the speaker can test the acoustics of the hall and the sound system, too, if he is making use of it. When there is preliminary business to be transacted before the speech, the chairman should discuss with the speaker whether he wishes to be on the platform for this part of the meeting or whether he will wait offstage or among the audience.

If this last method is adopted, when the moment for the speech arrives the chairman must leave the platform, escort the visitor back to it and introduce him to the audience. Some inexperienced chairmen conclude the preliminary business and then say, 'We will now ask our guest speaker to come to the platform and I will leave you to him.' The chairman vacates the platform and the unfortunate speaker then has to mount the stage, set out his notes and take charge of the audience, doing the best he can to restore the situation after this discourteous introduction.

Unless there is some special reason, such as a slide show, for the chairman to sit among the audience he should always stay on the platform or at any rate no further away than the front row. In a public meeting, especially when the topic is controversial, the chairman must certainly remain on the platform. With a non-controversial subject and a small audience he might decide that after making the introduction he can leave the speaker alone on the platform, providing he can resume his place beside the speaker with no delay at the end of the talk. If the chairman remains on the platform, he inevitably becomes part of the show. He must therefore remain still and attentive to the speaker throughout, doing nothing to distract the audience's attention. A chairman has been known to nod off during a dull speech. If he is prone to this, he would be better to doze in the front row than on the stage! However, for meetings of any size and importance he will certainly remain beside the speaker.

His presence there should ensure good order and the smooth running of the meeting. A chairman, by virtue of his office, in a sense symbolizes the organization he is serving. Its dignity, status and efficiency are represented by him. The public image of a society, club or other institution is impaired if its chairman is manifestly weak and ineffective. Therefore the quality he most needs to display is authority, though this should be quiet and unobtrusive. A bossiness which antagonizes those present is the last thing one wants in a chairman: his task is to guide and control the meeting, enabling the speakers to make their points as effectively as possible. He must not use his position as an opportunity to show off his own personality.

The chairman of a society or club whose purpose is primarily social has a fairly straightforward job when there is a guest speaker. He welcomes him before the meeting, introduces him graciously to the audience, supervises the question-and-answer session, voices the audience's thanks (unless someone else has been deputed to do so), adds his personal thanks and escorts the visitor from the hall. He may of course offer the visitor entertainment and refreshment before he leaves, but this would depend on circumstances and the persons involved. During the period when questions can be put to the speaker, someone has to call the questioners, selecting who is to be asked to speak if several hands are up. This is a natural role for the chairman, but he might arrange before the meeting that the speaker himself will direct this session, inviting the questions and choosing the questioners. In this case the chairman announces at the end of the talk that the speaker has agreed to answer questions and he calls for someone to open the proceedings. If no one offers, then he should have a question of his own ready to start things off. After this, more questions will follow and the speaker can take over. On the other hand, the chairman may prefer to direct this session himself and, except in the smallest meetings, it is desirable that he should. He can be expected to know more than the visitor about the members of the audience who may wish to ask questions: some will need encouraging; others containing, if not downright suppressing. It is also easier for him than for a visitor gently to restrict the number of supplementary questions and ultimately to bring the meeting to a close.

At a large public meeting, particularly when something controversial is to be discussed, the chairman's task is harder. Here his authority is all-important. Passionate speakers from the platform and eager questioners – and hecklers – from the body of the hall can quickly raise the temperature of the meeting, and while such excitement can be stimulating, it can also lead to bad tempers and disorder. This can be prevented by a chairman whose authority is respected and who can defuse a threatening situation with a humorous remark or a well-phrased appeal to the audience's sense of responsibility. It is very much a matter of personality.

With several speakers to be heard, and then questions and perhaps short speeches from the floor to follow, much will depend on the chairman's sense of timing. He should make it clear to the speakers beforehand how long each is permitted to speak and he should ensure that no one is allowed to over-run. It is only fair to a speaker to give him a warning that his time is running out. In some venues, such as those which house political or trade union conferences, there is a system of lights to indicate to the speaker that he must wind up or stop. A simpler method is to put a card, marked for example 'two minutes', on the table in front of the speaker. For the apparently unstoppable orator, the chairman will be forced to stand up and intervene, doing what he can to avoid giving offence to the speaker and his supporters, but being absolutely firm that he cannot bend the rule about timing for one particular speaker.

At annual general meetings, the chairman himself may have to make a speech of some length, outlining the progress of the organization in the last year. In addition to this, he must fulfil his customary role of enabling each item on the agenda to be dealt with adequately and allowing each person his say, while at the same time keeping up the momentum of the meeting so that it does not become bogged down by one perhaps not very important point. This really does need skill and tact, for people do not like to feel they are being rushed when important matters have to be considered. On the other hand, the majority of those present will feel frustrated if a few individuals insist on wrangling at length over trivial points. The chairman who sits back and allows this to continue unchecked has only himself to blame if people begin to leave the meeting before some important proposals have been discussed. How to check such an exodus depends on local circumstances and the chairman's assessment of the persons involved. One way is to suggest that the meeting will probably want to move on to the next item in ten minutes' time at the most and speakers should therefore limit their remarks to essential points. Another is to say that only a certain number of speeches will be allowed before a vote is taken. If the chairman is uncertain how this will be received he can put such a guillotine procedure to the vote. If it is carried, he knows that he has the backing of the majority for such action.

As can be seen, the chairman's job is challenging and demanding, not least because he must be able to think and act quickly, reacting to impromptu remarks and unforeseen occurrences. A good voice and presence are valuable assets, as are a temper that cannot be ruffled and a sense of humour. Courteous always, he must nevertheless leave no doubt in anyone's mind that he is the person in authority and that his rulings 'from the chair' must be respected.

6 Your Voice

31 You and your voice

You and your voice are unique. Even if another speaker used exactly the same material as you, your talks would be different because your personalities and voices are different. Voice and personality are intimately linked. We can judge a great deal from a person's appearance, and especially his face, but we cannot really know the kind of person he is until we hear his voice. As a public speaker you are presenting not only your material but also your personality to the audience, and the chief vehicle of this is your voice.

Since sincerity is a prime necessity for successful public speaking, it follows that you have to accept your personality as it is and your voice too. Any attempt to develop a new voice for yourself, one which does not match your innate personality, would be a foolish waste of time. Yet accepting the kind of voice you have is not the same as believing it is incapable of improvement. While our voices serve us well enough for daily conversation at home and at work, comparatively few are of sufficient strength and clarity to communicate easily with an audience in a large hall. If you are going to be a public speaker, you must assess your voice with cold detachment, seeking the aid of tape-recordings and the advice of honest friends. The chances are that you will be forced to recognize that the speech sounds and vocal quality which are perfectly adequate for communication in everyday life will not be good enough for addressing an audience for a substantial length of time. English speakers are very prone to the habit of moving their organs of speech as little as possible: their lips barely open, jaws remain stiff, tongues rise and fall as little as possible to shape a sound. The practice of vigorous speech is underdeveloped.

Much of our vocal quality depends on our upbringing. We copy the voices of our parents and close members of our families and these are conditioned by the region and environment in which we live. It is natural to speak like those around us and it is interesting to notice the extent to which people adapt their mother tongue to a new accent when they move to a different area where the same language is spoken. The Englishman who emigrates to America finds it easy to modify his accent to bring it closer to the sounds he hears around him. Yet people from a country whose native language is not English rarely lose their foreign accent completely no matter how long they live in England or America. This is because the native speech habits they learnt as children in order to form the sounds characteristic of their mother tongue are so deeply implanted that they are almost impossible to eradicate.

Such speech habits have now become a part of you and you have subtly modified them over the years to express your personality. To try to change them completely in order to become a public speaker would be unreasonable and self-defeating. What would be worthwhile, however, would be to identify where your voice can be improved in clarity, quality and strength, without losing the aspects that make it uniquely 'you'. In other words, there should be no question of learning a special voice for public speaking, different from your usual one. Accept your own voice and train it to be as effective as you can make it.

Any discussion of speech invariably comes around to the question of accent. Can a speaker with a marked regional accent be as successful as one who speaks RP (Received Pronunciation – also known as Standard English). The answer must surely depend on the audience being addressed and the nature of the topic. In this latter part of the twentieth century, all kinds of accents are acceptable, where thirty years ago they would have been resented or rejected, and many public speakers use a modified local accent. Some speakers of eminence almost flaunt their personal and idiosyncratic accents – it is very much part of them and we accept them as such. If you are new to public speaking and are unsure about your accent, ask yourself to what extent it is likely to be a barrier to your communication with possible audiences. It would be a mistake to try to change your accent completely, but if your accent is very strong, it is possible that two or three characteristic sounds might need to be modified to enable you to communicate more readily with audiences beyond your own locality.

Whatever your personal speech is like, an understanding of basic voice production and voice control must be of advantage to a person who is to speak in public. There are many skilled teachers and excellent books which deal with this in detail, but here is an outline of the subject with some simple exercises that can be used to improve one of the speaker's principal resources – his voice.

The voice

To create vocal sound, the breath passes under pressure through the approximated vocal cords in the larynx. The vibrating vocal cords create sound waves which are given their different sound qualities by the speech organs – lips, tongue and jaw – as they pass through the mouth. The sound is amplified by several resonators, principally the chest, pharynx and nasal cavities.

Breath

Breath is the motive power of the voice and a breath supply which is poor or inadequately controlled produces weak, uncertain tone and phrases that trail away at the end. On the other hand, a good supply of breath, managed with understanding, is the prime source of vocal energy, giving strength to the voice and confidence to the speaker. For ordinary conversational purposes, comparatively shallow breathing will suffice, but for the special requirements of a public speaker a much fuller use of the lungs should be cultivated. In the course of speech you will only occasionally need to be consciously managing the breath. Your mind will be chiefly on your audience and on what you are saying. But exercises will increase both your breath capacity and your control, and so give you the basis for good tone production, which will become second nature and which you can rely on without conscious thought.

Breathing exercises should be done regularly but for short periods of time only. (Some people feel faint if they practise deep breathing for too long at a time, so be warned.) Without going into great anatomical detail, we can consider the chest as a cavity containing the spongy lungs that expand as they fill with air and contract as air is expelled. The cavity is bounded by the ribs at the sides and front and back and by the diaphragm at the base. The diaphragm is an elastic muscle which is dome-shaped. When a breath is taken, the ribs move out and the diaphragm flattens, thereby increasing the area of the chest cavity and giving the lungs plenty of room to fill with air. On breathing out, the ribs and diaphragm return to their original position, thus providing a way of controlling the emission of breath. For ordinary speech purposes deep breathing involving noticeable movement of the ribs and diaphragm is not required, but the public speaker may need this additional power source and should learn to use it.

Relaxation

The management of the breath involves a delicate balance between tension and relaxation. Certain parts of the speech mechanism will be under considerable tension (the vocal cords are one example) while other parts must be relaxed, since tension of the wrong kind will cause strain, tiredness and a poor sound. Therefore even a short session of practice should be preceded by simple relaxation exercises. You particularly need to get rid of the tension in the shoulders, neck, face and head; but relaxation is a matter of the whole body and relaxation exercises are best done lying on the floor. There should be no problem about this in the privacy of your room, but if you want to do some exercises just before your speech or in any place where lying down is not possible, there are some exercises which can be done in a sitting position or even standing up.

Exercise

Lie flat on the floor wearing loose clothing. Consciously let the floor take the weight of all your body. Then tense and relax each part in turn. Begin by stretching each arm up above you in turn, tensing the hand and fingers and then removing the tension from the fingers, hand, wrist and finally the arm, so that it flops back to the ground where it will lie relaxed beside you.

Now stretch the legs and point the toes. Bend the feet firmly downwards so that they are fully stretched. Pause and then slowly remove the tension from the toes, feet, ankles and legs, so that they are now as relaxed as the arms.

Tense and relax each part of the trunk as you move up towards the shoulders, which you should lift off the floor, tensing and rounding them before allowing them to relax and return to the floor once more. Now rest for a minute or so and enjoy the relaxation. Then quietly work on the neck and face muscles. Start by turning the head to one side so that the tension is felt on the other. Return the head to the central position so that this tension is relaxed. Repeat to the other side. As you lie there, tense and relax the facial muscles, starting from the scalp and moving downwards. Wrinkle the brow into a deep frown and then relax the wrinkle away. Screw up the eyes and then open them slowly and gently. Wrinkle the nose and relax it. Draw the lips into a tense grin and then allow them to return to relaxed normality. Slowly open the jaw and release it back to a closed position of rest. Do all this in a leisurely fashion, allowing yourself pauses between each act of tensing. When all the body is relaxed, lie quietly at rest, breathing gently.

At first, when you are unaccustomed to releasing your tensions in this way, you may find that the period of relaxation becomes irksome after a fairly short time and you will wish to be up and doing. This is an indication of the stress to which you have become accustomed. With regular practice you will find you can increase the period of relaxation, with resulting benefit to yourself. Some people find soothing music helps them to relax more completely, for relaxation is as much a mental process as a physical one. Quiet thought-pictures with pleasant associations are therefore a useful adjunct to the exercises.

When you rise from the floor, do not undermine all the good you have achieved by moving hastily. Roll over slowly on to one side, draw up the knees and, pressing with the hands, come up into a kneeling position. From there, slowly rise to your feet, unrolling the body and head into a well-balanced upright position.

If it is not convenient for you to lie on the floor for your relaxation exercise, then sit upright on a firm chair which will support your back. The activity of alternately tensing and relaxing various parts of your body, as described above, can be adapted to this position, though it is obviously less suitable than lying on the floor.

Time may not always permit a leisurely session of relaxation. Just before a speech, for example, one or two relaxation exercises are very valuable, but they may have to be done standing up in a greenroom or a cloakroom. Similarly you may have only limited time to do some breathing practice and so will want to precede it with relaxation exercises that can be carried out in a short time. For such occasions make use of the following exercise which is done in a standing position.

Exercise

Stand up straight with the feet slightly apart and the body well balanced. Stretch the arms above the head as far as possible, tensing the fingers upwards. Stretch the head back to look at the ceiling. Hold this position for a few seconds, feeling the tension. Then consciously relax the muscles, starting at the fingertips, letting them curl down. Let the hands and wrists relax, so that the hands droop. Next the tension is taken from the arms so that they drop to the sides; the shoulders become rounded and the head drops forward. The whole body now bends slowly from the waist and the arms dangle loosely as though they were a puppet's. From this relaxed position, slowly return to an upright posture.

After this general relaxation session, it is useful to apply a more localized relaxation to the shoulders and head before you begin breathing exercises. Make sure the shoulders are free by rolling them forward and back, moving them easily and avoiding any vigorous action. It is essential for good breathing that the shoulders are not raised nor held stiffly. Therefore be sure to relax them before you begin breathing exercises. Move the head easily from side to side and then drop the head forward so that the point of the chin touches the chest. Slowly circle the head, so that at the mid-point the chin is pointing upwards, after which it completes the circle to return to its starting place. Repeat in the other direction.

Finally, before you begin your breathing exercises, balance the body well on your two feet, placed slightly apart. Ensure that the head is not poked forward and that the shoulders are not pulled back like a guardsman's on parade. A natural, easy, alert posture with the head, neck and spine in alignment is what is required.

Breathing

To make full use of your lungs' capacity, you need to allow them room to expand. Do not think that breathing in means sucking in large quantities of air. (Over-inflating the lungs is as undesirable as having too little breath.) Think rather of opening out the rib-cage and giving the lungs room. As soon as you do this, nature will quickly fill the vacuum thus created with air. You will have taken the necessary breath without trying! There will be no noisy inhalation nor apparent effort, apart from moving out the ribs. Here is how to do it:

Place your hands flat on the sides of your ribs. Swing out the ribs against your hands, which will allow you to feel the movement and how far your ribs are moving. Your lungs are now filled with air. Hold the position for a count of three and then allow the ribs to return to rest as the breath is expelled. Let the air enter the lungs through a slightly opened mouth as well as the nose and be sure not to heave the shoulders up when the breath comes in. Concentrate on the firm outward and slightly upward movement of the lower ribs. You may not feel a great deal of movement in the ribs at first, but with a few regular daily exercises you should find the expansion increasing.

The ribs move not only at the front and sides, but also at the back. Put your hands where the back of a waistcoat would be and again swing out your ribs. See if you notice a movement in these ribs at the back. At first you may detect very little movement but practice should increase it.

When you breathe in this way, you are conscious of the rib movement but cannot see the diaphragm which is also moving inside your body. As already explained, its slight dome shape is flattened as the ribs expand and the air enters the lungs. You will, however, detect one effect of the movement of the diaphragm and that is a slight drawing in of the wall of the abdomen. In non-technical language this means that strong muscles of the abdomen have taken a hold on the diaphragm and are in a position (in conjunction with the rib muscles) to control the pressure of air on the vocal cords. This fact is of the greatest importance to singers and, although public speakers do not have to manage their breath so consciously and constantly as a singer, they should understand the process, as it is the foundation of good voice production.

Strong and satisfying vocal tone begins with the application of steady air pressure on the vibrating vocal cords. As the air in the lungs begins to be used up, the pressure has to be maintained by the controlled return of the diaphragm and ribs. There is an analogy with the bicycle pump: if you put your finger partly across the outlet hole and press the plunger down the tube, you can maintain the air pressure on your finger even though the quantity of air in the tube is decreasing every moment. If, as a public speaker, you allow your ribs to collapse too rapidly, your vocal tone will be shallow and breathy and you will be forced to use short phrases punctuated by frequent breaths. When you practise the exercises below, try to be conscious of the rate of collapse of your ribs and, if necessary, regulate their return to a position of rest. A few minutes a day given to these exercises will increase your breath capacity and control.

Exercises

1. Take a breath as already explained, hold it for a count of three and then breathe out to a count of three.
2. Take a breath slowly by expanding the ribs to a count of four. Hold it for a count of four. Breathe out to a count of four. In due course you can increase the count to five or six. (You can do this exercise when out walking – breathing in

for four paces, holding it for four paces and breathing out for four paces; rest for a few paces and repeat.)

3. Take a breath and hold it for ten or fifteen seconds before breathing out. Some people can hold their breath for a minute or more; others for only a short time. Find your own normal duration and then, in regular practice, try to extend it as your muscles come more under control. *Never* force yourself beyond what is comfortable, however.

4. Take a breath and say the letters of the alphabet loudly and clearly, getting as far as you can in one breath *without* forcing yourself on with splutterings and gaspings. As practice develops, try to increase the amount you can say in one breath. As a variant of this, instead of saying the alphabet, count out loud up to, say, thirty or as far as you can easily get. Yet another exercise is to expel the air with a hiss, timing how long you can keep a *steady* sound going.

Exercises are one thing and performance is another. The aim of exercise is to strengthen your capabilities so that you do not need to think of them when you are actually speaking. All the same, there are times when a conscious use of techniques you have practised in your exercise sessions become necessary. One would be when, for a special reason, you wished to deliver two or three sentences in one breath or when a particularly impassioned plea demanded extra vocal force. This would be the time to think about your method and bring into play a technique used by singers and actors. This consists in not allowing the ribs to fall during exhalation until the last possible moment and controlling the air pressure with a firm but gentle squeeze of the abdomen. It is even possible to take an additional breath by relaxing the diaphragm while keeping the ribs out. This of course is advanced technique but, if you are interested, you can try it out for yourself when you feel you have made progress in your basic breathing exercises. It cannot be too much stressed, however, that this is for rare occasions only and that natural control of exhalation by the flexible return of the ribs is what is usually needed for public speaking.

The larynx

The larynx (or voice box) contains the vocal cords and this is the one part of the speech mechanism that is not subject to the speaker's conscious control. All sorts of things can affect the vocal cords adversely – tense muscles in the neck and head, a stiff jaw or badly managed breath, not to mention colds, sore throats, tiredness and strain induced by shouting and other abuse of the delicate mechanism. There are a great many things that can go wrong, but happily it is not difficult to do the right thing, providing we have not grown too accustomed to tensions and other forms of vocal abuse. In serious cases remedial treatment may take a long time and will need specialist advice. However, it is comforting to remember that the vocal cords are very tough and when used correctly can stand long and vigorous use: just think of the pressure per square inch that an opera singer puts on his cords!

The function of the vocal cords in speech and song is for them to come into close proximity at the top of the windpipe, so that when air under pressure is applied to them, it forces itself between them and sets up vibrations which create sound waves. As the cords shorten in length, the pitch of the resulting sound is raised higher; as they lengthen and thicken, the pitch drops lower. Fortunately these minute adjustments are made for us by mental processes. It is not possible for us to lengthen or shorten our vocal cords consciously and directly, so for practical purposes you can forget them.

The resonators

The vocal sound issuing from the larynx would be as unimpressive as the sound of a violin without its belly or a trumpet without its bell, were it not for the resonators in the human body. These are the cavities in which the sound waves set up sympathetic vibrations which greatly enrich and amplify the original sound. The principal resonators are the pharynx, the mouth and the nose. The first two can be altered in shape and size; the nose cannot.

When the shape of the cavity is altered by changes in the position of the mouth and the tongue, then a sound characteristic of that shape is produced. This gives us the great variety of vowel sounds. For example, a wide open mouth and a flat tongue produce the vowel *ah*, while an almost closed mouth with the lips spread and the front of the tongue held high gives us the *ee* sound. For effective speech, you should be firm and vigorous in using the lips, tongue and jaw in making the various vowel shapes, without going to the extreme of 'mouthing' the words.

Vocal energy originates from the pressure of air at the larynx. Take a breath correctly, with the ribs swung out and raised, and say cleanly *a-egg-egg-egg*. Be quite gentle with this exercise; do not exert too much pressure, for there must be no suggestion of an attack on the vocal cords but rather a firm smooth action like engaging a gear on a car. The sensation is akin to saying *pah* with the lips. In this exercise do not stop the breath too abruptly but prolong the vowel for a second or so to enable you to notice the firm clear tone you produce. This is because your vocal cords are closely approximated and all the breath is being turned into tone. There is no question of holding this tone back in the throat; it moves forward brightly and easily. What is more, the sound waves thus created will be invoking the appropriate resonances in the mouth and nasal cavities as required. There will be no need to 'place the voice' in various parts of the mouth and the head – it will be done for you. What you have to do is to breathe correctly, cultivate an open throat, a loose jaw and flexible lips and tongue, and conceive of your sounds as being initiated (as indeed they are) at the larynx. In your mind visualize them being formed towards the back of the neck behind the larynx. From there they move out freely through the open throat, gaining their character and resonance from the flexible speech organs and resonating cavities as they go. That is the theory: here are some exercises to help you put it into practice.

1. Always begin with **relaxation** and **breathing** exercises as already described.

2. Open throat. Yawn deeply and feel the sensation of openness at the back of the mouth and throat. Another suggestion is to imagine a ping-pong ball made of air resting on the back of your tongue. In your imagination push it back down your throat. Again you should have a wonderful sense of openness. This exercise is meant to show you how much more space you have in your throat than you normally use and to exercise the muscles that can maintain the openness for you. As in all vocal exercises, do not go to extremes. A throat forced open to its fullest extent can feel stiff and awkward when you come to articulate. Use your own wise judgement.

3. Articulation. Take a breath by expanding the ribs and allowing the diaphragm to descend, at the same time opening the throat as in (2) above. This process can be combined by 'yawning in a breath'. Then practise these sequences *gently* but firmly. It must be stressed again that there should be no sense whatsoever of attacking the vocal cords, but simply a smooth clean movement. So yawn in a breath, keep the ribs out, pause for a second and then say (with a clear gap between each sound):

> *a-egg-a-egg-a-egg-a-egg*
> *a-eye-a-eye-a-eye-a-eye*
> *ah-oh-ah-oh-ah-oh-ah-oh*
> *ee-aw-ee-aw-ee-aw-ee-aw*

Make up similar sequences of single vowel sounds for yourself. Remember not to chop off the vowel too quickly. Enjoy the sound of it!

This articulation exercise will not transform your speech overnight, but if you practise it regularly, you should become increasingly aware of the clean, bright sound of which your voice is capable.

To maintain this tone quality when you have to initiate the sound with a consonant rather than a vowel is the next stage. The best consonants to begin with are K and G. Try saying:

> *a-keg-keg-keg-keg*
> *gig-gag-gok-gook*

Then introduce different consonants into the sequences given above. (See also section 8, on consonants.)

4. The tongue. For the production of vowel sounds, the tip of the tongue should be just touching the back of the front teeth. Practise placing it there in a relaxed fashion. The tongue can be an unruly member, wanting to go anywhere except where you wish it to. You certainly do not want it to be humped up or pulled towards the back of the mouth when you are making an open sound. For instance, its position for *ah* is flat along the bottom of the mouth. You can gain some control over it in exercises such as these: push the tongue out and retract it three or four times; push it out and move it from side to side, then up and down, finally bringing it back to rest on the bottom of the mouth with its tip behind the bottom front teeth.

Beyond this it is best not to worry too much about the tongue, except to encourage the tip to stay down when a vowel is being made. When making consonants, the tongue is often very active indeed, as explained later in section 8.

5. The lips. The Englishman's traditional stiff upper lip, however admirable in moments of crisis, is definitely not an asset for his speech. Lips need to be flexible and the upper lip tends to be more set in its ways than its lower partner. Make them both work by pursing them together and then pushing them forward and around as if chewing with a closed mouth. Then spread the lips wide in a grin and push them forward into an O shape. Invent your own exercises for inducing vigorous movement with the lips in open and closed positions. Be sure to make the upper lip do its fair share.

6. The jaw. The lower jaw is capable of considerable movement – far more than most of us use and far more than is actually necessary for clear speech. All the same, the habit of speaking with a stiff jaw and through teeth and lips that hardly open at all is very common and will not do for a public speaker. Just to see how much (or how little) you open your jaw, try saying *ah* in front of a mirror. Then put two fingers on their sides into your mouth and see how much wider the opening has become. Now say *ah* again with this wider opening and notice the improvement in quality. Of course in connected speech it is not always necessary to open the jaw to its fullest extent even for the *ah* vowel. But being aware of the advantages of a freer and wider jaw movement will enhance the clarity of the speech, partly because the actual shapes of the vowels will be more efficiently made and partly because the sound is not bottled up behind narrow teeth and lips. To loosen the jaw try these exercises. Put your fingers below the ears on the places where you can feel the movement of the lower jaw away from the upper. Gently drop the point of the jaw to its fullest natural extent. Do not force the jaw but allow it to assume its fully open position easily. Repeat the exercise two or three times. Then move the jaw from side to side in both the open and closed positions.

With an open throat and an easily moving jaw, you are well placed to produce vocal tone of a very good quality.

7. The vowels. It is a common belief that clarity of speech depends very largely on the consonants. One hears people complain (and rightly) of indistinct consonants, particularly at the end of words, and there is a feeling that if speakers would only spit out their consonants all would be well. (This ignores the fact that many consonants cannot be spat out at all!) Undoubtedly there is much to be said for clear articulation of the consonants, but vocal tone is carried chiefly by the vowels. For clear and expressive speech it is necessary for each vowel to be well shaped and hence differentiated. The natural tendency of many English speakers to move the speech organs (lips, tongue and jaw) as little as possible results in blurred sounds and a lack of well-contrasted vowels.

The vowels you use will be natural to your own accent, which may very possibly be a regional one modified by Received Pronunciation. There is no point in a book of this kind in giving an elaborate description of how each vowel is formed in Received Pronunciation, with exercise to match; there are several manuals on the subject for those who are interested. Some sentences containing the principal vowel sounds of English are given below, so that you can consider how you personally pronounce each vowel. You can check that you are making full use of your speech organs in forming them and, if you are not entirely satisfied, you can experiment to find a better way. A tape-recorder will be of great use here. The ultimate test will be the distinctness and tone quality of each sound that you are studying.

As you practise each sound sequence, remember your previous exercises on relaxation, breathing and articulation, and make use of them. First say each vowel on its own and then speak the sentences:

EE and IH. *Need he really think that she is eager to see his feet?*
(Are you spreading the lips sufficiently for this sound?
Could the forward part of the tongue be higher?)

EH. *The red pen is not very heavy, so lend it to Fred.*

AE. (as in *hat*). *Gladys was sad that the cat had vanished from the mat.*
(The jaw opening for this vowel should be quite wide.)

ER. *The bird on the fir heard the mirth of the earth.*

UH. *Some will hurry to come among us.*

AH. *The far part of the garden is where the farmer leaves his cart.*
(Some speakers pronounce the r sound in these words. If you wish to eliminate it, see that the tip of the tongue is not allowed to rise while the vowel is sounding.)

O. (as in *stock*). *The dog has lost its bone in the frosty trough.*

AW. *Gordon was appalled at the thought that this course would ignore the law.*

U. (as in *book*). *He put his foot on the book but could not fully reach the nook.*

OO. *Lou will have to move her boots and shoes away from the food.*
(Nowadays this sound is usually preceded by a short 'ih' sound, so that for 'true' we say 'trih-oo' rather than 'troo', thus making the sound into a diphthong.)

Diphthongs are vowels made up of two elements and therefore they involve a movement of the speech organs when the sounds are being made. You will see this most clearly if you look in a mirror and say '*Oh!*' A great difference to the pronunciation of such vowels can be made by a very slight shift of one or other of the elements.

AY. *Dave will pay as much as May to dance in the waves all day.*

OH. *Don't row the boat so slowly when you go to Hove.*

I. *I will find you a pie that is as high and as wide as the sky.*

OW. *Now the mountain frowns down on the town.*

OY. *The boys were annoyed and made a noise because they no longer enjoyed their toys.*

Here are some sentences where several different vowel sounds are used. Practise reading them aloud, concentrating on making well-formed and clearly differentiated vowels, but without sounding stilted and unnatural.

> *With a deep breath, he took his pen in his hand and was ready to write.*
>
> *The loss of her dog was sad, for she said what a friend he had been to her.*
>
> *The pool was so cold that I could not put my foot in it without a shudder.*
>
> *I would rather face the full consequences of my deed than tell the truth to my father.*
>
> *How will the news be told to the old man before it travels all around the town?*

8. Consonants. These sounds are made when the speech organs interrupt in some way the free flow of the breath. This can be complete, as when the lips are brought together in the formation of p, or partial, as for example with s. An efficient use of consonants gives shape and definition to spoken words and these qualities are lacking if the tongue moves lazily or the lips are only partly closed when they should be fully closed. In a big hall a speaker really does have to make his consonants tell. In a small place, however, over-deliberate consonants become an affectation and should be avoided, though with most speakers there is less danger of this fault than of their being content with consonants lacking in vigour and distinctness.

As with vowels, a full treatment of the many consonants we use can be found in manuals of speech training. Here, however, are some sentences designed to exercise tongue, lips and jaw in the production of clearly enunciated consonants. Try looking in a mirror as you speak these sentences and see if you think there is sufficient movement of your speech organs. Say the sentences in a whisper sometimes, so that everything will depend on the vigour of your consonants in getting your meaning across. Tongue twisters are excellent practice, so we begin with the most famous of all:

Peter Piper picked a peck of pickled peppers from his Papa's pocket.

Beatrice and Bertha both beat the bad boys with their brooms.

Ten tall tenants told the tyrant what to do.

Down in Dorset, darkness doesn't daunt us.

Can you get a keg of ale, clear and cool, with a golden glow?

Five very fat families filled our village to overflowing.

The thieves gathered all that they could and then hid themselves in the thick thickets.

(If the 'th' sound in 'thieves', 'thick' and 'thickets' is indistinct, make sure the tip of the tongue is brought between the teeth to form this consonant.)

Soon the summer will smile on the lazy pleasures of swimming and sunbathing

After church we lunched cheaply on chops and cheese.

Many and mighty were the men from the mountains who came riding and singing into our town.

32 Care of the voice

The speaker's voice must be one of his most treasured possessions and, as such, it must be taken care of. The vocal mechanism is a paradox: it is both tough and yet extremely delicate. It is tough enough to stand up to a life time of normal use, yet so delicate that it can be ruined for professional purposes by the time the speaker is thirty. It all depends on how the voice is used and how it is cared for.

Apart from serious disease, what is most destructive is forcing the muscles of the voice. This may be done in an ignorant attempt to gain more power when the wrong muscles of the neck and throat are tensed. It may come about when the voice is tired after a long session and the speaker insists on continuing to use the weary organ at full blast. Unnatural shocks to the voice such as frequent bursts of sudden shouting, at a football match for instance, will strain the muscles and put the voice in danger. A public speaker has to be conscious of these things and cosset his voice, though the first essential is to make sure that his breath control and voice production are correct and easy. If he is aware of tensions and the onset of tiredness in the early part of his speeches, it would be sensible for him to consult a voice teacher and follow the advice given.

If you are going to undertake a long speech in public for the first time (or after a long break from public speaking) you should prepare the voice by warm-up sessions spread over the preceding days, gradually lengthening the time you talk continuously. This is only commonsense. No athlete would dash out on to the track to run a mile without proper training. He knows very well that if he did his muscles would seize up and his stamina would be non-existent. Similarly, the voice needs to get into training for a long speech and there should be warm-up exercises immediately before the event. Of course it is perfectly possible to speak for two hours without any preparation whatsoever. But you would do so at your own risk and you should not be surprised if you have a sore throat the next morning! It is well-known for teachers who speak all day to their classes of pupils to complain of vocal tiredness at the beginning of term. After the holiday break their voices are not geared up to the task of speaking for several hours a day and it takes a while for them to get back into their vocal stride. Similarly a singer who undertook a heavy dramatic role immediately after a holiday when he had not been practising would be in grave danger of losing his voice.

It is best to avoid long periods of informal conversation before a speech. Chatting can be very tiring indeed and is all the more undesirable if it takes place in a hot and smoky atmosphere. The enemy of vocal health is anything that dries the throat, and hot rooms and tobacco smoke will do just that. Drinks do not help a great deal beyond giving a very short-term relief, because the vocal cords are most effectively lubricated by secretions in the larynx itself. If for any reason they dry up, then the voice is like a car engine running without oil.

Colds and the attendant mucus seem to produce too much lubrication and it is tempting to buy medicines to 'dry up' these fluids. Speakers should avoid these completely. They certainly dry up the annoying mucus, but some preparations also dry up the natural secretions that lubricate the vocal cords, and although the speaker may think he has achieved some temporary relief, he has actually succeeded in removing the oil from his vocal engine.

There is no known cure for a cold, so if it is essential to speak when you have a cold, one can only advise using the voice most carefully and cutting the speech as short as possible before retiring to bed with an aspirin and a hot drink. Forcing the voice to speak vigorously while you are suffering from a cold may well bring on a sore throat and laryngitis. Pending medical advice, the great essential is not to use the voice at all. Very often the only treatment your doctor will prescribe is complete rest for the voice, together with soothing inhalations of steam. If you insist on speaking at length with a bad laryngitis, you could put your voice out of action for weeks. Smoking, heavy drinking and living in a hot, dry atmosphere are all thoroughly unhelpful for this condition.

You may have done all the right things by way of vocal preparation, but still experience a dry throat just before you begin to speak. This is the unfortunate effect of nerves; it is perfectly natural, very common and just what you do *not* want to have! Control of nerves along the lines suggested in Chapter 2, 'Your nerves and you', will help you avoid the symptom, but if it does occur, sucking a sweet or a blackcurrant pastille should overcome the dryness and enable you to make a start.

A healthy way of life, fresh air, no tobacco and alcohol only in moderation – these are a good foundation for vocal health, as well as general physical well-being. Beyond this, the speaker should learn to use his voice correctly, avoiding strain and fatigue and any tendency to 'force' it.

33 Microphones

A microphone of quality, used correctly, can be a good friend to a public speaker, but one that is faulty or used badly will be more trouble than it is worth. So many problems can arise with mikes that some public speakers have only one piece of advice about using them – don't! One can see their point: a microphone is no guarantee of audibility. Just think of the meaningless blur that issues from so many loudspeakers in use at railway stations. All of us can recall occasions when the strong voice of the speaker became a light echo of its former self when the microphone broke down and left him unaided. A faulty adjustment can make it howl unbearably, and people can trip over the cables and knock it over. The comic possibilities of a microphone that slowly slides down its stand and forces the speaker to bend over it ever lower and lower are well-known to comedians. The more one thinks about mikes the more they seem fraught with horrid dangers.

Yet, when installed and used correctly, a microphone and its associated sound system can be a really valuable resource for a speaker in a large hall. If it is suggested that you might wish to use such apparatus, the wise response is to say you would like to try it out in advance before making up your mind. For this you will need friends in various parts of the hall who will report honestly on how your voice is coming across. One of the first things to establish is how near the mike you should stand. If you are too close, your voice is likely to sound muffled or else it will boom unnaturally. If you are too far away, it will not be picked up at all. You are already meeting one of the difficulties in using a microphone, namely the limitation it places on your movements. A microphone in a fixed position decrees that you must stand still with it in front of you. Anything beyond the smallest movement puts you in danger of being 'off-mike' with a consequent loss of audibility. Perhaps this is no bad thing, for a lecturer *should* stand still. But there are occasions when movement is necessary.

This problem can be solved by using the mike which is hung

around your neck or clipped to a lapel, or one that is held in the hand. The former is very successful in removing the feeling of constraint from a speaker; he can move his head and body quite freely, the mike does not come physically between him and his audience and the only extraneous problem he has to be aware of is the lead from his microphone to its socket.

A hand-held microphone has advantages over a fixed one, but it does restrict the use of the speaker's hands. It is easy enough to use if he needs to move about the platform, pointing to visual aids, for instance (again providing he does not trip over the cable, and it is handy for slide presentations when he wants to be able to turn freely to and from the audience and the screen. But if the speaker wishes to use notes or to pick up exhibits, he has only one hand free. Moreover the microphone will always be a prominent feature of his general appearance. There is a temptation to hold it right in front of the mouth (as many pop singers do) and this intrusion blocks off part of the speaker's face from the audience. A lapel microphone or one hanging around the neck can be inconspicuous and is clearly preferable.

As a visiting speaker, you should not be bothered with the technicalities of the sound system, unless of course you are bringing your own. However, it is worth mentioning that a strident howl may alarm you when your microphone is switched on. This is caused by the microphone being placed too near one of the loudspeakers and the 'gain' on the amplifier being turned up. Increasing the distance between the microphone and the loudspeaker and turning back the 'gain' control will cure this. It is something to listen for if you are walking around the platform with a mike in your hand: if you are walking towards a loudspeaker, you and your audience may receive a noisy reminder that, in one sense at least, you have gone too far.

Try to solve all these problems before the meeting begins. It weakens the opening of your talk if you have to tap the mike to make sure it is working (and it is not good for the mike either) or – worse still – if you say a few words and then call out, 'Is the mike working? Can you hear me at the back?' If you follow previous speakers, you should have a good idea about the quality of the sound system and the effectiveness of the microphone. You may have to readjust the stand to suit your height when it is already switched on. Handle it gently to avoid unwelcome clicks and bangs being amplified around the hall, and never forget that a live mike will pick up asides muttered to yourself or to others on the platform – you may not want everyone to hear them!

The speaker's bookshelf

However good your public library may be, you will want to have at least a few books beside your desk for ready reference when you are preparing your speeches. Presumably the books relating to your special interests are already on your shelves; but what else would you find useful when you sit down to draft the talk?

A good dictionary is an essential. No one is going to check your spelling, but if you value precision in your use of language you will want from time to time to verify the exact meaning of a word that seems to suit your needs. What is more, one word leads to another: a word in the dictionary definition may be preferable to the one you had in mind. Even more helpful in this pursuit of the best word is a Thesaurus. The best-known was originally compiled by Peter Mark Roget in the mid nineteenth century, and there are numerous modern editions. *The Penguin Pocket English Thesaurus*, edited by Faye Carney and Maurice Waite, is based on Roget and incorporates an index of some thirty thousand words. Suppose, for example, that you were at a loss for an alternative to the word 'fluent' (an appropriate one for a public speaker): the index would refer you to five different entries, from which you would cull 'articulate', 'eloquent', 'well-turned', 'felicitous', 'expressive', 'wordy', 'verbose', 'communicative', 'having a way with words', 'loquacious', 'voluble', 'garrulous', 'prolix' . . . an ample choice! Under the subheading of 'lecture' it gives 'orate', 'sermonize', 'pontificate', 'speechify' and 'spout' – a sobering list for public speakers!

For general knowledge and quick reference for facts and dates you need a compact one-volume encyclopaedia. There are several on the market to choose from: a useful and well-established one is Hutchinson's *New Twentieth Century Encyclopaedia*; an alternative is the *Macmillan Encyclopaedia*.

A well-chosen and apt quotation can make a good opening or conclusion to a speech and a source book of such remarks would be worth having. One to be recommended is *The Penguin Dictionary of Quotations*, compiled by J. M. and M. J. Cohen. The same authors have also put together a *Dictionary of Modern Quotations* (also published by Penguin Books), drawn exclusively from the twentieth century. Also available is *The International Thesaurus of Quotations* (Penguin Books).

Those speaking on political topics should find invaluable the *Guide to Political Quotations* by Caroline Rathbone (Longman). Collections of humorous stories can also be found in bookshops, but it is better if you compile your own selection from newspapers, books, radio and television. The advantage of this is that you will be choosing the kind of humour that most appeals to you and that you will enjoy re-telling.

Few of us can be confident about the many terms used in modern philosophy, politics, arts and science. A really excellent companion, which explains about four thousand of them, is the *Fontana Dictionary of Modern Thought* edited by Alan Bullock and Oliver Stallybrass (Fontana/Collins).

If you want to take further your studies in the understanding and practice of the voice, one could recommend *Voice Production and Speech* by Greta Colson (Pitman) and *Your Voice and How to Use it Successfully* by Cicely Berry (Harrap). A very useful book with a great deal of practice material packed into its fifty-nine pages is *Speaking with a Purpose* by Christabel Burniston (English Speaking Board).

FOR THE BEST IN PAPERBACKS, LOOK FOR THE

In every corner of the world, on every subject under the sun, Penguin represents quality and variety – the very best in publishing today.

For complete information about books available from Penguin – including Pelicans, Puffins, Peregrines and Penguin Classics – and how to order them, write to us at the appropriate address below. Please note that for copyright reasons the selection of books varies from country to country.

In the United Kingdom: For a complete list of books available from Penguin in the U.K., please write to *Dept E.P., Penguin Books Ltd, Harmondsworth, Middlesex, UB7 0DA*

In the United States: For a complete list of books available from Penguin in the U.S., please write to *Dept BA, Penguin, 299 Murray Hill Parkway, East Rutherford, New Jersey 07073*

In Canada: For a complete list of books available from Penguin in Canada, please write to *Penguin Books Canada Ltd, 2801 John Street, Markham, Ontario L3R 1B4*

In Australia: For a complete list of books available from Penguin in Australia, please write to the *Marketing Department, Penguin Books Australia Ltd, P.O. Box 257, Ringwood, Victoria 3134*

In New Zealand: For a complete list of books available from Penguin in New Zealand, please write to the *Marketing Department, Penguin Books (NZ) Ltd, Private Bag, Takapuna, Auckland 9*

In India: For a complete list of books available from Penguin, please write to *Penguin Overseas Ltd, 706 Eros Apartments, 56 Nehru Place, New Delhi, 110019*

In Holland: For a complete list of books available from Penguin in Holland, please write to *Penguin Books Nederland B.V., Postbus 195, NL–1380AD Weesp, Netherlands*

In Germany: For a complete list of books available from Penguin, please write to *Penguin Books Ltd, Friedrichstrasse 10 – 12, D–6000 Frankfurt Main 1, Federal Republic of Germany*

In Spain: For a complete list of books available from Penguin in Spain, please write to *Longman Penguin España, Calle San Nicolas 15, E–28013 Madrid, Spain*

PENGUIN REFERENCE BOOKS

The Penguin English Dictionary

Over 1,000 pages long and with over 68,000 definitions, this cheap, compact and totally up-to-date book is ideal for today's needs. It includes many technical and colloquial terms, guides to pronunciation and common abbreviations.

The Penguin Reference Dictionary

The ideal comprehensive guide to written and spoken English the world over, with detailed etymologies and a wide selection of colloquial and idiomatic usage. There are over 100,000 entries and thousands of examples of how words are actually used – all clear, precise and up-to-date.

The Penguin English Thesaurus

This unique volume will increase anyone's command of the English language and build up your word power. Fully cross-referenced, it includes synonyms of every kind (formal or colloquial, idiomatic and figurative) for almost 900 headings. It is a must for writers and utterly fascinating for any English speaker.

The Penguin Dictionary of Quotations

A treasure-trove of over 12,000 new gems and old favourites, from Aesop and Matthew Arnold to Xenophon and Zola.

The Penguin Wordmaster Dictionary   Manser and Turton

This dictionary puts the pleasure back into word-seeking. Every time you look at a page you get a bonus – a panel telling you everything about a particular word or expression. It is, therefore, a dictionary to be read as well as used for its concise and up-to-date definitions.

FOR THE BEST IN PAPERBACKS, LOOK FOR THE

PENGUIN REFERENCE BOOKS

The Penguin Guide to the Law

This acclaimed reference book is designed for everyday use, and forms the most comprehensive handbook ever published on the law as it affects the individual.

The Penguin Medical Encyclopedia

Covers the body and mind in sickness and in health, including drugs, surgery, history, institutions, medical vocabulary and many other aspects. 'Highly commendable' – *Journal of the Institute of Health Education*

The Penguin French Dictionary

This invaluable French-English, English-French dictionary includes both the literary and dated vocabulary needed by students, and the up-to-date slang and specialized vocabulary (scientific, legal, sporting, etc) needed in everyday life. As a passport to the French language, it is second to none.

A Dictionary of Literary Terms

Defines over 2,000 literary terms (including lesser known, foreign language and technical terms) explained with illustrations from literature past and present.

The Penguin Map of Europe

Covers all land eastwards to the Urals, southwards to North Africa and up to Syria, Iraq and Iran. Scale – 1:5,500,000, 4-colour artwork. Features main roads, railways, oil and gas pipelines, plus extra information including national flags, currencies and populations.

The Penguin Dictionary of Troublesome Words

A witty, straightforward guide to the pitfalls and hotly disputed issues in standard written English, illustrated with examples and including a glossary of grammatical terms and an appendix on punctuation.

FOR THE BEST IN PAPERBACKS, LOOK FOR THE 🐧

PENGUIN DICTIONARIES

Archaeology

Architecture

Art and Artists

Biology

Botany

Building

Chemistry

Civil Engineering

Commerce

Computers

Decorative Arts

Design and Designers

Economics

English and European
  History

English Idioms

Geography

Geology

Historical Slang

Literary Terms

Mathematics

Microprocessors

Modern History 1789–1945

Modern Quotations

Physical Geography

Physics

Political Quotations

Politics

Proverbs

Psychology

Quotations

Religions

Saints

Science

Sociology

Surnames

Telecommunications

The Theatre

Troublesome Words

Twentieth Century History